DR DAVID MARTYN LLOYD-JONES

DR

DAVID MARTYN

LLOYD-JONES

Dr Eryl Davies

PUBLISHING WITH A MISSION

EP BOOKS
Faverdale North
Darlington, DL3 0PH, England

web: http://www.epbooks.org

e-mail: sales@epbooks.org

First published 2011
Second impression 2012

British Library Cataloguing in Publication Data available

ISBN-13: 978-0-85234-760-7   ISBN-10: 0-85234-760-X

Printed and bound in Great Britain by the MPG Books Group.

Contents

Dr David Martyn Lloyd-Jones

PREFACE

It has been a privilege and joy to write this brief and 'popular' biography of Dr D. Martyn Lloyd-Jones. Repeatedly while preparing this biography and rereading what Lloyd-Jones wrote, I have been deeply challenged and humbled both as a Christian and as a preacher.

The Lord gave me the privilege to sit under his ministry on numerous occasions in churches and in the Bala Ministers' Conference annually. He was a friend and a pastor, dearly loved and appreciated by many younger and older pastors, particularly in Wales. We are deeply indebted to him.

My prayer is that the Lord will use this biography to encourage and constrain many of us as believers to know and enjoy the Lord more, as was his experience. Will one or more of the readers of this book also feel a conviction and burden to pray earnestly to the Lord for revival and to encourage others to do so? That would be a cause for rejoicing and thanksgiving on my part.

May the gracious, covenant-keeping God of our fathers be merciful to us in our day and grant a powerful outpouring of the Holy Spirit upon the church to his eternal glory in Christ.

D. Eryl Davies
Cardiff
September 2011

INTRODUCTION

Unexpected? Yes. Unwelcome? Certainly! Dr D. Martyn Lloyd-Jones was dismayed by what was happening. The date was 14 December 1926, and the national newspapers had printed startling headlines concerning him: 'Harley Street Doctor to become a Minister' and 'Leading Doctor turns Pastor'. For two days, Lloyd-Jones' family home in London was besieged by newspaper reporters who all waited in vain to interview him. Lloyd-Jones even refused to pose for a photograph. There were good reasons for his negative response. He was essentially a shy man and disliked the publicity intensely. But more to the point, he had not yet informed his employers at the hospital of his decision to leave medicine to become a church pastor. And they were not pleased to hear the news first from the newspapers.

Yet there was a deeper reason for Lloyd-Jones' dismay at this unexpected publicity. For him, the newspapers could not understand why he was leaving the medical profession, especially when he was set for a brilliant medical career and then only twenty-six years of age. The press was only interested in news, and the more sensational it was the better. However, the living God had been dealing with Lloyd-Jones, and he had felt an irresistible call from heaven to preach the gospel of Christ. He did not expect unbelievers to appreciate this fact either.

The background to this extensive publicity is interesting. Only a few days earlier on Saturday 27 November, Lloyd-Jones had arrived by train at Aberavon/Port Talbot station in South Wales after a four-hour journey from London. It was a dark, uninviting evening. At the railway station, awaiting their distinguished guest, were three local men. One was Mr E. T. Rees, the church secretary of Bethlehem Forward Movement Presbyterian Church, Sandfields, Port Talbot, and he was accompanied by a church member and the church's previous pastor. They extended a warm welcome to Lloyd-Jones as he was due to preach in their church the following day, with a view to becoming their new pastor.

On the next day, his preaching was well received. In fact, when Lloyd-Jones said after the evening service that he had felt drawn to the church and the locality despite its poverty and high unemployment, the church members were delighted. Events moved quickly over the following days. At a Church Committee Meeting on 1 December 1926, the minutes read: 'All members expressed their admiration for, and delight with, Dr D. M. Lloyd-Jones and the Committee unanimously resolved to recommend his name to the church as prospective pastor.' A further visit was arranged for Sunday 12 December. The response of the church to Lloyd-Jones' preaching on this second occasion was unanimous: they wanted him to be their pastor! This was the story that leaked out to the newspapers and caused Lloyd-Jones such dismay and annoyance.

We must now retrace our steps and look at Lloyd-Jones' background before describing his work as a pastor in Port Talbot and then later in Westminster Chapel, London.

But I must offer one word of explanation before proceeding. In the early chapters when describing his childhood and youth, I have used his first name to indicate the way his family and friends referred to him. Later, rather than using an abbreviation like 'ML-J' or 'L-J', I have consistently used the name 'Lloyd-Jones' or occasionally 'Doctor' to refer to the subject of this biography. The latter term was used by many of his friends and others to express their affection and respect for him, and he accepted its use both in public and in private. Interestingly, he refused to accept any honorary degrees or titles because of his high regard for the degree of Doctor of Medicine (MD) which he had been awarded by the University of London for his medical research before entering the Christian ministry. He was a real 'doctor'!

1

THE EARLY YEARS

David Martyn Lloyd-Jones was born in Cardiff, South Wales, on 20 December 1899. He was the second of three sons born to Welsh-speaking parents, Henry and Magdalene Lloyd-Jones, who were both from the western area of Cardiganshire, Wales. In Cardiff, Henry ran his own grocery shop. However, there were two problems over the following five years which made him relocate to west Wales.

One problem was the business itself, for he struggled to obtain an adequate profit margin in order to support his growing family. The other problem was more personal. Henry was convinced that city life did not agree with his health, and that he needed to live in a rural area like west Wales. Consequently, when Martyn Lloyd-Jones was five years old, the decision to leave Cardiff was made.

Llangeitho

The family settled in the village of Llangeitho in west Wales, where the main occupation of people of that area was farming. Llangeitho was famous especially for its religious history in the eighteenth century because Daniel Rowland (1711–1790), an Anglican curate in the parish, had exercised a powerful and fruitful ministry from the 1730s. Some local revivals had also broken out there during Rowland's ministry, as in 1762. A year later, in 1763, Rowland was forced out of his parish work by the church authorities so a new church building was erected for him to continue his ministry, which became part of the Calvinistic Methodist movement and, later, a part of the Methodist denomination. Although Martyn's mother had an Anglican background, and his father was a Congregationalist, it was more convenient for them to attend this Calvinistic Methodist church in the village.

One of the immediate challenges for Martyn and his two brothers in moving to Llangeitho was that of learning the Welsh language, as their parents had spoken English to them while in Cardiff. One reason for this was the fact that Magdalene's mother had died when she was very young, and, when her father had remarried in her early teens, because her stepmother was English, the family's main language became English. This influenced the decision of Henry and Magdalene to speak English to their own children when living in the more anglicized city of Cardiff. However, within two years the children were fluent in the Welsh language.

Their home life was extremely happy and both parents were loving and hospitable as well as wise. His father's business was that of a general store in which he sold milk, cream and butter, but also various farming implements and machinery. There were regular visitors to their home, often because it was adjoining the shop. There was always a warm welcome awaiting them, and Martyn never forgot some of the more interesting characters who came to visit.

Apart from playing football with friends, there were other pleasurable activities for the young Martyn. For example, he enjoyed going on business trips with his father to the local farms, in the trap pulled by their own horse. During the school holidays, it was a sheer joy to be able to go to his maternal grandparents who lived on a large farm — Llwyncadfor — outside Newcastle Emlyn, only a few miles away. His grandfather's speciality was breeding and training horses for regional and local shows in which they often won major prizes. Here Martyn helped feed the horses and occasionally walked them to a horsebox or to the railway station ready for travel to a show.

Incidents

There were, however, some significant incidents in his early years that left an impression on him. One was the fire which destroyed their home and shop in January 1910, when Martyn was only ten years old. His mother and older brother were away at the time, but as the fire and smoke spread throughout the house, Martyn and his brother Vincent were woken by their father in the early hours of the morning. His father, Henry, threw Martyn out through the upstairs window into the arms of three men waiting to catch him below. A ladder was then used for his brother and father to escape through the same window. It was a remarkable escape and Martyn never forgot it.

Soon after this incident, a new teacher in the local school rebuked Martyn for not concentrating on his studies. If he did not study adequately, he was warned, then he would fail to obtain a scholarship to the County Intermediate School in nearby Tregaron. Those remarks challenged the young boy deeply. He had heard confidentially from his grandfather the unwelcome news that his father was experiencing financial difficulties in his shop and would probably become bankrupt. He kept this information to himself, but it meant that a scholarship was essential if he was to progress to the Tregaron School, as his father would be unable to pay the fees. His mind was made up. He would now concentrate on his school studies. And his hard work was rewarded; over a year later he won the coveted scholarship he desperately needed.

Tregaron

When, at the age of eleven, the time came for him to transfer to the more senior school in Tregaron, the thought filled him with considerable dread. This was because he was required to stay in lodgings there from Monday to Friday, even though it was only four miles away. He hated the idea as he was so happy at home. Despite his brother Harold already being there, Martyn's three years in the school were very unhappy. His longings to be home with the family were deep and painful. However, he made good friends, enjoyed the lessons, and developed a good friendship with his brother. In the summer term, his parents allowed him to walk or ride his bicycle home each weekday rather than stay in Tregaron. He enjoyed that immensely! When his younger brother, Vincent, also started at the school and the three brothers shared the same lodgings, it was easier for him to cope with homesickness.

It was during the year of 1913 that Martyn decided on a future career in medicine. The factors influencing the decision are unclear, although the fact that his great-grandfather had been a doctor may have had some bearing. Or it may have been a local young man he respected, who, after qualifying, returned to his home area to practise medicine. Whatever the influences, Martyn's parents encouraged him in achieving his ambition.

1913 was important for another reason too. The Association of Calvinistic Methodist Churches in South Wales held its summer meetings in Martyn's home church in Llangeitho. And there was a special reason for this location. The Association was celebrating the bicentenary of the birth of Daniel Rowland. Many people flocked to Llangeitho for these meetings which were held over a period of four days. Some famous preachers of the day belonging to the denomination were booked to preach, and, in order to accommodate the crowds, a stage which included a pulpit was erected in a field together with many benches for the four thousand or more people to sit on and listen to the preaching. The meetings left a deep impression on Martyn and aroused an interest in the early Calvinistic Methodist leaders. This interest continued and deepened throughout his life.

Only a few months later in January 1914, however, their tranquil family life in Llangeitho was broken. It was a Sunday evening and the family were sitting together at home relaxing, when Henry informed the children of his desperate financial situation and the need for them to relocate. Martyn had already heard of his father's financial difficulties from his grandfather and Henry was grieved to know he had been carrying the burden of that knowledge for some time.

As the two older boys needed to complete their studies until the summer, Henry decided the family could stay local to Tregaron while he went to Canada to secure work for himself and a home for the family. Soon he sailed for Canada, but by early summer he recognized that he had failed in his quest, and so he was left with no other alternative but to return and try to find work and a home in London.

2

LIFE IN LONDON

It was Martyn whom his mother decided to send to London to meet her husband in early August. Martyn would also help his father in the search for a suitable business and home. It was a wise arrangement as she and the other two boys would stay with her parents in Llwyncadfor. More practically, it would be easier for relatives in London to give temporary accommodation to Martyn and his father.

On Saturday 1 August 1914, Martyn set out by train on the long journey to London where he was met by his uncle. Two days later, his father's ship reached Plymouth, and he completed his journey by train to London where Martyn was eagerly waiting for him.

Unknown to them, the following weeks were going to be demanding and frustrating, but for Martyn it would also be fascinating as they searched for a home and a business which his father could purchase. It would be a long process and only in October, eleven weeks later, were the family reunited in their new home in 7 Regency Street, Westminster.

War

Germany had declared war on France only two days after
Martyn had arrived in London, and, on the following
day, Germany invaded Belgium. The British Government
felt it had no choice but to honour an 1839 Treaty which
guaranteed the neutrality of Belgium, so on 4 August the
Prime Minister, Herbert Asquith, formally declared war
against Germany. It was a difficult period for the Liberal
Government too as three of its ministers resigned.

Martyn, therefore, had arrived in London at a critical
time in the nation's history. But there was also fascination
for him. For example, he had the opportunity to attend the
House of Commons over the following weeks and years to
hear some of the important debates there. There were times,
too, when he and his father stood outside 10 Downing Street
and saw leading politicians like Asquith entering and leaving
the famous residence. It was an unforgettable sight.

On the London streets, there were many military
personnel with the crowds singing and clapping whenever
they saw a regiment of soldiers march past. In the
excitement, many young men walked together cheering as
they made their way to the nearest recruiting office to enlist
for military service. However, by the end of August 1914,
the stark realities of the war began to be felt by the people.
British troops fighting alongside their French and Belgium
allies were forced by the Germans to retreat from Mons. In
doing so, they suffered very heavy casualties. Economically,
the bank rate soared and the Stock Exchange was closed
while long queues of people outside the Bank of England
tried to exchange their banknotes for gold. The euphoria
amongst the people regarding the war quickly evaporated.

Reunited

In their search for a home and a business, father and son walked many miles and read carefully all the advertisements in newspapers and in shop windows. The first weeks were discouraging. There seemed no possibility for Henry to secure a suitable property. One major problem was that he had no money to place as a deposit in buying a business. Just as disappointing was the fact that no relative would agree to provide him with a loan. Eventually, he discovered a dairy and milk business being sold more cheaply for a quick sale due to the war conditions, and with a loan of £50 from a friend in Wales, he was able to pay the deposit and secure the business and the accommodation above the shop. This was exactly what he needed for himself and his family. One can only imagine the joy they all felt to be reunited once again that October.

Because of his financial difficulties, including debts and the need to establish his business, Henry decided to keep Martyn and his younger brother home from school that autumn term. Indeed, his financial situation seemed so bleak at the time that, despite receiving an excellent report from the school at Tregaron on Martyn's examination performance in the previous summer, he doubted whether he could afford to send him and Vincent to a London school. For the following weeks they were kept home to assist in the business, with Martyn often delivering milk in the early mornings.

The business soon began to prosper and a relieved father saw it was possible for the younger boys to resume their education, this time at Marylebone Grammar School in January 1915. However, Martyn was needed regularly to deliver milk at 5.30am before going to school, and he was also required to help in other ways.

London life

Life was full for the teenage Martyn. One of his delights was to sit in the Strangers' Gallery in the House of Commons, either with his brother Harold or on his own, and to listen to some of the important debates. From their home, the House of Commons was only a brief walk, and in 1915 the coalition government was struggling to lead the country.

In December 1916 one of the government ministers, the Welshman David Lloyd George, a favourite with Martyn, became the new Prime Minister, succeeding Herbert Asquith. Relations between the two politicians had been strained for a period and Asquith believed there was a conspiracy against him in which his successor played no small part. There was further drama in October 1919 when Lloyd George's coalition government was defeated in Parliament, leading to his resignation. It was such occasions, and others like the Irish debates leading to independence for Ireland (excluding the six counties in the north which remained under United Kingdom rule) in December 1921, which would have attracted Martyn to the House of Commons.

Another activity for the teenager was attendance with his family at their Welsh language Presbyterian church (or its other name, Calvinistic Methodist) in Charing Cross. The church was well attended and provided for the religious and social life of Welsh exiles. The minister, Peter Hughes Griffiths, was an attractive character who appealed to

Martyn because of his originality and independence. From 1917, possibly one of his favourite meetings in the church was the Sunday school adult class led by an eye surgeon, Tom Phillips, who encouraged open discussion on key subjects. It was Dr Phillips' daughter, Bethan, whom Martyn was to marry later.

In the summer of 1916, Martyn's examination results were impressive as he had passed with distinction in most subjects. On his own initiative, he had already written to some hospitals enquiring about studying medicine, and thus he chose to sit an entrance examination to the nearby St Bartholomew's Hospital. Following an interview with the Dean, Martyn was accepted at the age of sixteen for medical studies.

Medicine

Dating as far back as AD 1123, St Bartholomew's Hospital is the oldest hospital in England. Catering originally for the poor and sick in the heart of the city of London, its history is impressive and fascinating. In 1546, Henry VIII refounded the hospital and guaranteed its future by an endowment. A medical school was established in 1843 and over the decades the hospital gained considerable prestige for the quality of its training, research and clinical excellence. In recent years, the hospital has specialized more in cardiac and cancer care.

It was in this famous hospital that Martyn Lloyd-Jones received his medical training. Despite the war conditions, he was excused from military service due to the fact that there was a serious shortage of medical doctors. Martyn settled well into hospital life and enjoyed his studies immensely.

His hard work was amply rewarded, and it was in 1921 that he obtained the degrees of M.R.C.S, L.R.C.P, M.B. and B.S. with distinction in medicine. He became Sir Thomas Horder's junior, then Chief Clinical Assistant, and also assisted him in his demanding Harley Street private practice. He achieved the much coveted M.D. (Doctor of Medicine) degree from the University of London at the age of only twenty-three, and then the M.R.C.P. when he was twenty-five. Martyn had also been encouraged by Horder to undertake research into a cardiac condition, which he completed.

The influence of Sir Thomas Horder (later Lord Horder) on Lloyd-Jones cannot be overemphasized. Promoted to be the Queen's physician, Horder was an outstanding physician much sought after by the rich and famous. A rigorous thinker, he took pains to collate and analyse all the available data before making his diagnosis.

Even during his studies and medical success, Lloyd-Jones enjoyed classical music, occasionally opera, and especially going to hear important debates in the House of Commons. At home, he often delivered milk before going to the hospital and went regularly with his family to their Charing Cross church, where he and his family had become formal members in 1914. Here he had been Superintendent of the all-ages Sunday School for a year, and he spoke occasionally in various meetings. It seemed to most people and even to Martyn himself for some years, that he was a Christian. But that was to change as Martyn came to see himself in a new light.

3

BECOMING A CHRISTIAN

Whether or not a person is converted gradually or suddenly, quietly or more spectacularly, was later unimportant to Lloyd-Jones. What was more important was that the person had become a Christian, however long or short it took. How then did Martyn become a Christian?

It was over a long period in his early twenties that God dealt with him. However, there had been a number of significant factors beforehand which had been influential and preparatory to him becoming a Christian. It is these factors and influences we now need to identify in order to see how God worked in his life.

Influences

To have been rescued in such a remarkable way from a blazing house fire in Llangeitho when only ten years of age brought home to him in some degree a sense of the transitory nature of human life. Again, at the age of thirteen, those memorable Association meetings in Llangeitho of the Calvinistic Methodists left a deep impression upon him. This was the first time he witnessed open-air preaching and saw such large congregations. He was overawed too by some of the famous Welsh preachers in those meetings. He had one vivid memory in which one preacher used the illustration of electric tramcars and the need for them to be connected to electricity before they would be able to move. This was used by the preacher to highlight the power of God and the need of the church to seek that divine power. That was an emphasis Lloyd-Jones retained throughout his own ministry.

Only a few weeks after the Association meetings, his school teacher gave him a booklet outlining the life and work of the Welsh exhorter, Howell Harris (1714–1773). Harris had been one of the men God used in Wales from 1735 in what had been a major revival in that land. Here was the gripping story of a young man who came to know the living God and his amazing love in Christ for sinners. Repeatedly, Harris knew the Holy Spirit coming upon him and giving him profound experiences of the Lord. His preaching ministry was extremely fruitful. This booklet, therefore, gave Lloyd-Jones some awareness again of the greatness of God.

On relocating to London, the family attended the Welsh Calvinistic Methodist Church where, at the age of fourteen, Martyn and his family became church members. Although Martyn was not a Christian at the time, he was nevertheless sincere in what he was doing. He writes: 'For many years I thought I was a Christian when in fact I was not. It was only later that I came to see that I had never been a Christian and became one. But I was a member of a church and attended my church and its services regularly.'

Sadly, the biblical emphasis on the holy character of God, the fact of human sin, and the need to be reconciled to God through the substitutionary death of the Lord Jesus was a message Martyn rarely heard in his or other churches, either in Llangeitho or in London. Too often the preachers assumed that all those in the congregation were already Christians.

At the age of seventeen, he was reading the Bible regularly and with increased understanding. And it was at this time he recognized the biblical teaching that God controls the universe and is working his purpose out in all the affairs of individuals and nations. That includes also those whom God chooses to be saved. Consequently, the biblical term 'predestined' became important to him, and he loved to share this truth with others.

Only a year later, in 1918, tragedy struck the family when his older brother Harold died. Martyn and Harold had had a close relationship, but both were victims of the flu epidemic in which many people died. Harold never recovered and died at the young age of twenty. One can only imagine the impact of Harold's death on Martyn himself. Four years later their father died which left another huge gap in family life. Henry Lloyd-Jones, despite his earlier financial problems, had made a success of his London business. He was a kind and wise man who cared deeply for his family.

Sin

It seems that from about the age of twenty until he was twenty-five, God dealt with this medical student deeply and personally. Sin began to trouble him more. He was able to see plenty of evidence around him of the fact that people were sinful. There were, for example, the desperately poor people living in close proximity to the hospital who needed medical help. Their lives were often given over to satisfying their own sinful lusts and desires. He could not ignore the grip that sin had on their lives. In this way he came increasingly to accept that man's nature is not essentially good or even neutral but rather biased and disposed towards sin. But he saw this also with regard to the rich and the famous whom he helped to treat either in the hospital or in Lord Horder's Harley Street consulting rooms. Education, money, fame, and even the status of royalty, did not deal with man's basic problem of sin and estrangement from God.

But this observation was confirmed in his own life as his sense of personal sin and guilt before God deepened. Although a faithful church member and living a decent, respectable life, he now knew the inwardness of his own sin and the powerful lusts which prevailed there and longed for gratification. He recognized he was as much a sinner as anyone else.

But as God dealt with him, he realized that his spiritual condition and need were desperate. He was troubled by his experience of sin ruling his life. Years later, he expressed this in his own words:

He brought me to know that I was dead, 'dead in trespasses and sins', a slave to the world, and the flesh, and the devil, that in me 'dwelleth no good thing', and that I was under the wrath of God and heading for eternal punishment. He brought me to see that the real cause of all my troubles and ills, and that of all men, was an evil and fallen nature which hated God and loved sin. My trouble was not only that I did things that were wrong, but that I myself was wrong at the very centre of my being.

Clearly conversion for Lloyd-Jones was not sudden but gradually built up over several years. Now, however, it was reaching a critical period.

Another influence on the young medical doctor was in listening to the preaching in Westminster Chapel, especially when their new minister came in 1923. He was Dr John A. Hutton and his preaching appealed immensely to Lloyd-Jones, even though he did not expound the Scripture. However, he brought home again in a different way to Lloyd-Jones the immense power of God and his ability to change the lives of men and women, no matter what their condition or needs were. He also talked about the need for new birth. God was using this as well, to give Lloyd-Jones confidence in the living God and the hope that he too could be changed.

Saved

By the Easter of 1925, he had become a Christian. God had saved him. At home in a small study which he shared with his younger brother, Martyn experienced an overwhelming sense of the love of God towards sinners mediated through the Lord Jesus Christ. He now knew that he was forgiven and accepted by God because the Lord Jesus had borne all the guilt and punishment of his sin when he had died on the cross.

This was to be the central theme of Lloyd-Jones' preaching and work over the following years. It was the good news of the gospel. Quoting John 3:16 and 1 Peter 2:24, he declared years later:

Here is the Gospel... He saves us by bearing our punishment and by taking our guilt upon him. God smites him and the law of God is satisfied ... The Lamb of God has come. God has provided his own sacrifice. It is his own Son. This is what happened on Calvary's tree. God took your sins and mine and he put them on the head of his own Son and then he smote him, he punished him, he struck him, he killed him. The wages of sin is death.

As Lloyd-Jones discovered, religion or church attendance do not in themselves bring us into a right relationship with God. Listen to his warning:

Many people come to listen to the gospel who have been brought up in a religious atmosphere, in religious homes, who have always gone to church and Sunday School, never missed meetings; yet they may be unregenerate. They need the same salvation as the man who may have come to listen, who has never been inside a House of God before. He may have come out of some moral gutter; it does not matter. It is the same way, the same gospel for both, and both must come in the same way. Religiosity is of no value; morality does not count; nothing matters. We are all reduced to the same level because it is 'by faith', because it is 'by grace'.

4

CALLED TO PREACH

Even prior to Easter 1925, Lloyd-Jones had a conviction that he should be a preacher one day. There were hints that as a teenager he had felt this pull, and certainly he had had a sense of the call to preach the gospel before he became a Christian. However, after his conversion in 1925, this call to the Christian ministry became much stronger and persistent. In fact, it was difficult, indeed increasingly impossible, for him to push this conviction out of his mind though, as we will see, he endeavoured to do so.

Decision

After an address he gave in his own church one weeknight in February 1925 on 'The Tragedy of Modern Wales', he wrote to his close friend Ieuan Phillips, who would become his brother-in-law. By now, the relationship between Ieuan's sister, Bethan, and Martyn Lloyd-Jones was gathering momentum.

Lloyd-Jones was able to open his heart to Ieuan and describe how he felt regarding reactions to the address to his church. But he also shared in this letter concerning his own personal future: 'I have already made up my mind as to my future, in fact I did it as soon as I finished with the exam', that is, the examination he had for the degree of Membership of the Royal College of Physicians (M.R.C.P.) which he was awarded in April 1925. In the light of his decision to enter the ministry, Lloyd-Jones had already started learning New Testament Greek and he wanted Ieuan to send him some of the Greek examination papers used in the Entrance Examination to the Presbyterian Church of Wales's own Theological College in Aberystwyth. Lloyd-Jones was now serious in his resolve to prepare for a preaching ministry.

This was followed a couple of months later by an interview with the Principal of the Theological College, Dr Owen Prys. The latter was pleased to meet the young doctor and the interview was extremely amicable. However, on his return journey to London, he felt it was inappropriate for him to pursue a full-time theological course. His reasons were clear. He viewed his medical training, with its rigorous diagnostic approach, as an invaluable preparation for preaching. For him, too, a minister is essentially a preacher and pastor who is called and gifted by God. Lloyd-Jones was also persuaded that academic theological training can spoil gifted preachers in several ways. For example, such training placed too much emphasis on formal qualifications. Even worse, the training was dominated by liberal theology in university faculties and in most denominational seminaries.

Doubt

Unexpectedly, during the following months Lloyd-Jones struggled with doubts concerning his call to preach. Had

God really guided him to preach? Or should he remain in medicine? Some church leaders whom he respected either suggested he should stay in medicine or combine medicine and preaching. It was a confusing period for him in which he had little peace of mind. He speaks of going through a 'great crisis' in which he changed his mind in preference for staying in medicine. For months, even after his change of mind, this conflict regarding his future career troubled him. And in his struggles with the issue, he lost weight. But the world of medicine continued to attract him with its challenges and opportunities for research and clinical practice. He knew he could help people medically.

Confirmation

Once again, however, God guided and spoke to him by means of several incidents. He recalled one incident at this time when a married couple wanted him to accompany them to a London theatre. He agreed, but on coming out of the theatre at the end of the play, he noticed a Salvation Army band in the street playing hymn tunes. At that moment he realized that these were the people he belonged to, rather than those in the world. It was a profoundly significant moment for him.

Slowly, he also began to realize the emptiness of the world of medicine and unwittingly his boss, Sir Thomas Horder, was instrumental in this. Occasionally, Sir Thomas invited Lloyd-Jones to accompany him to special medical dinners attended by prominent medical doctors. They were interesting evenings as he was introduced to a wide circle of medical experts. What saddened him, however, was the attitude and language of these people. They seemed full of jealousy and were often critical of colleagues. Their world seemed empty and dissatisfying, holding no appeal whatsoever for the young doctor. He felt he had no affinity with these people.

On another occasion, the same lesson struck him but in a different way. While working in his research room, Lloyd-Jones was visited by one of his hospital chiefs who was distraught and simply sat by the fire in the room for a couple of hours without speaking a word to his junior. The lady he loved had just died, and he was overwhelmed by sorrow and loneliness. His world was empty now, and, despite his medical fame, he was helpless in the face of death. And he had no hope. This incident affected Lloyd-Jones deeply.

Obligation

But there were other factors too that began to impress upon him the call to preach. He was more aware, for example, of an *obligation* to preach the gospel to people. Whether it was seeing the people on the streets of London, or staff and patients in the hospital, he felt a responsibility to share with them the gospel by which he himself had been saved. The apostle Paul's words in Romans 1:14 express his feelings well: 'I am a debtor both to Greeks and to barbarians, both to wise and to unwise.' In addition, he was increasingly aware of the spiritual needs of his patients in the hospital. He felt a constraint to tell people of the gospel which they had a right to hear. Whether rich or poor, famous or ordinary, all his patients needed to hear the gospel, for sin and death were their major problems. Only the gospel could help them. There was another aspect which was even more important: recognizing the amazing love of God in sending the Lord Jesus Christ, his only begotten Son, to die in the place of sinners. Lloyd-Jones felt constrained by such love to make Christ known to others.

The result was that by June 1926 his doubts concerning his call to preach had all evaporated. The struggles were over. Now, he had to prepare for a new career. His words are emphatic: 'Whatever authority I may have as a preacher is not the result of any decision on my part. It was God's hand that laid hold of me, and drew me out, and separated me to this work.' His sense of a divine call was tested a few weeks later. An Assistant Professor of Medicine informed Lloyd-Jones that his position would soon be vacant, and that he was certain to be offered the post. But he had no misgivings or second thoughts. God had called him to preach, and he now knew that for certain.

In describing in later years the call of God to the preaching ministry, Lloyd-Jones in his *Preaching and Preachers* draws upon his own personal experience. For example, he refers to a kind of inward pressure of which a person becomes increasingly aware. There is also a concern for people as well as recognition by others that a person has gifts appropriate for the preaching ministry. But the crucial test for him was a constraint to preach. A person can no longer remain in the secular work he has so much enjoyed previously, although this is accompanied by a deep sense of unworthiness and inadequacy in being called to such a glorious and onerous task. These tests mirror closely his own experience in 1925 and 1926.

Drawn to Wales

Events moved quickly over the final six months of 1926. His own minister at Charing Cross wrote to the Superintendent of the Forward Movement of the Presbyterian Church of Wales, which seemed an appropriate sphere of ministry for Lloyd-Jones. He felt drawn back to Wales, and he wanted to minister the Word in a poor and deprived community. The Forward Movement was still a young, fledgling organization which had been established by the denomination in the late nineteenth century in order to reach the unchurched people of Wales with the gospel, especially in the new urban, industrialized areas. The Movement had lost momentum by 1926, and there was an urgent need for gifted evangelists to preach regularly in the churches and halls which had been established. Much to the surprise of the Superintendent, here was a gifted and increasingly well-known medical doctor who was being drawn into that strategic work.

Progress here was slow, partly due to denominational procedures. Already Lloyd-Jones was refusing to train in the normal way for the Christian ministry by studying for the full period of time in Aberystwyth. Approved by the London Presbytery of the Presbyterian Church of Wales as a candidate for the ministry, it was arranged for him to preach in a Forward Movement church in Newport, South Wales, in early November 1926. Lloyd-Jones did not feel drawn to the church or the area as it was not the socially-challenging situation he longed to be in as a preacher. Then an invitation arrived from Mr E. T. Rees, secretary of Bethlehem Forward Movement Church in Aberavon, Port Talbot. As we saw in the Introduction to this book, he preached there in late November of that year and was attracted immediately to the church and its surrounding environs. It was exactly the kind of situation in which he longed to serve. Another preaching visit in December, this time accompanied by his fiancée, Bethan, confirmed his conviction, and the church unanimously called him to be their minister.

Bethan

Events had also moved quickly and significantly in his relationship with Bethan Phillips during 1926. They already knew each other well from their church context, and Lloyd-Jones had been drawn to her for some time, although he was several years her junior. Bethan had also commenced medical studies at the same time, but at the University College, London, rather than at St Bartholomew's.

Bethan was an attractive, intelligent young lady who had done well in her medical training. From Easter 1926, their relationship blossomed, and, later that June, Martyn would write to Bethan's brother, Ieuan, to share the news that they were to be married: 'I know that I am the luckiest man on the face of the earth at the present moment.' During the summer, Martyn, Bethan, and their respective families were back in west Wales visiting relatives. The couple, now engaged, had to visit many relatives and friends, but there was ample time for them to be on their own as they walked the hills, sharing together their desires and plans for the future.

Wedding

Lloyd-Jones was committed to completing his medical research in the hospital and this meant working at least until the end of December 1926. The pressures on him and his future bride were considerable in preparing for their wedding in London on 8 January 1927, in clearing his research room in St Bartholomew's Hospital, and also in ordering what they needed for their new home in South Wales. Following the wedding, they spent a two-week honeymoon in Torquay,

Devon. On returning to London, Martyn succumbed to influenza, so their starting date for ministry in South Wales had to be postponed a few days. They arrived in Aberavon on 1 February; there they were hosted for a few days by a church family until their new home was ready. A new and powerful ministry was about to begin which was to impact both the community and the church.

5

SETTLING IN SANDFIELDS

Bethan Lloyd-Jones remembered the occasion well in early February of 1927. She and her husband had travelled by train from London to Aberavon. It was raining when they stepped off the train, and they were taken by church members to the home of the Robsons, a church family, where they enjoyed hospitality for a week, until the church house was ready for them. They were well cared for and prepared for their new life in the locality.

The church had been established in 1897 by the Forward Movement which was the evangelistic wing of the Presbyterian Church of Wales; meetings had been held initially in the Sunday School. The main church building was erected in 1914 to seat four hundred people. About seventy people attended the Sunday morning service and a few more in the evening. Church membership stood at ninety and there was a crippling debt which the church had incurred in erecting the main building. In its short history, there had already been as many as six ministers, with the latter resigning because he found the work discouraging and the debt a massive hindrance. The church members were unclear themselves about the nature of the gospel, often identifying it with social, humanitarian and political action which Lloyd-Jones deemed inconsistent with a biblical, prayerful approach to the work. The Dramatic Society, concerts, jumble sales, sports club, and the Temperance League all ceased with immediate effect.

Bethlehem Forward Movement Church was the full name of the church, though its popular name in the locality was 'The Forward' or just 'Sandfields', the latter referring to the surrounding residential area which also included a council estate, industrial sites and the seaside resort with its sandy beach and promenade. There were many streets with their terraced houses around the church, but most of the people were poor and unemployed. Many of the young people who left school in 1922 were unable to obtain even one day's paid employment. Drunkenness, prostitution, gambling and crime were rife in the area. It was to this socially deprived and needy situation that Lloyd-Jones felt called to preach as an evangelist.

Welcome

The main 'Welcome Meeting' organized by the church for their new pastor was held a couple of days after their arrival, on Thursday 4 February, with crowded congregations for the afternoon and evening meetings. The local newspaper allocated two full pages to reporting the meetings under the title, 'Impressive Induction Services'. Lloyd-Jones' minister from London, the Rev. Peter Hughes Griffiths, preached in the afternoon from Esther 4:12–14. The evening service, chaired by the previous minister, Rev. T. J. Lewis, provided a 'history' of the call by the church secretary, E. T. Rees, while others commended and welcomed Lloyd-Jones before he was formally recognized as the new pastor of the church.

Because he lacked formal theological training, there was uncertainty in the denomination as to how Lloyd-Jones should be regarded. He had been 'recognized' only as a lay-pastor in the welcome services, but could he be ordained as a minister of the gospel? Was theological training essential when he already had a good grasp of the Bible and theology? He had also learned New Testament Greek while in London. Opinions were divided but eventually, in October 1927, he was ordained as a Presbyterian minister.

The task awaiting Lloyd-Jones in Sandfields was a formidable one. Reviewing the first seven years of his ministry in the church, the same local newspaper remarked that he was 'labouring in one of the most difficult fields of Forward Movement evangelism in Wales'. The paper then described the Sandfields area of Aberavon as a 'dead end' with its 'sandy wastes and dreary crowded houses which convey a sense of desolation, almost of hopelessness. What could a man denied work, disillusioned by social callousness, do here but live for a day, deteriorate, drift and die?' Into this 'desperate little world', Lloyd-Jones had come 'preaching, living the gospel of old-new hope'. This was an accurate description not only of the locality but also of the task passed down to the new pastor.

The man

What kind of man was this new pastor? He had some outstanding natural gifts, such as a strongly analytical and logical mind. He was renowned for his excellent memory and an eye for detail, yet he possessed an ability to identify easily the big picture in terms of principles. From his medical training, he brought his diagnostic approach to expose so easily the way in which churches, politicians and people in general were preoccupied only with the symptoms rather than the causes of their problems.

Lloyd-Jones was unassuming, yet an extrovert who possessed an abounding energy and an appetite for work and study. He also expressed a deep interest in people, although he could be forthright and impatient at times. His public speaking was marked by eloquence and a commanding, logical presentation of his material.

He loved the Welsh language and culture, especially its rich Christian heritage including hymns which he regarded as being far superior to those in the English language! One of his greatest joys was to be with his wife and children; it was with them that he was able to relax and experience considerable happiness as well as fulfilment.

Approach

For Lloyd-Jones, the major activities of the church would be the Sunday morning and evening services, an all-ages Sunday School, a Monday prayer-meeting, which, at the beginning, about forty attended, and a Wednesday Fellowship meeting. The new pastor held the latter as an open discussion of questions and difficulties relating to practical Christian living. He led this and the other meetings as well as the adult Bible class on a Sunday afternoon. He also held a Brotherhood meeting on Saturday evenings where he led a discussion more devoted to biblical and doctrinal teaching. Preaching and prayer were to become the main features of church life.

The terraced house which the church had bought for the use of their pastor was conveniently situated near to the church, and, in the opposite direction, it was only a few minutes' walk away from the beach. It was a three-bedroomed house, and one room downstairs was converted into a study by Lloyd-Jones. It was his custom to spend the mornings and several afternoons to prepare for his preaching, interspersed with times of prayer; here in the study, he would also counsel individuals, when necessary. Very soon, he was engaged most weeks in preaching in other churches on Tuesday and Thursday afternoons as his reputation spread.

Reading

He read the Bible daily and thoroughly, disciplining himself to read through the entire Bible once each year. He encouraged his congregation to do the same and provided them with his own scheme to assist them. In this early period, he soon discovered Rev. Robert Murray M'Cheyne's method which he had prepared for his Presbyterian church members in Dundee many years previously. Lloyd-Jones regarded it as being far superior. M'Cheyne (1813–1843) had prepared his scheme so that people would read four chapters from the Bible each day, which meant that within a year they had read the Old Testament once, and the Psalms and the New Testament twice. The preacher, according to the Doctor, should regard this as a minimum for his yearly reading of the Bible.

But there were other books too which the new pastor loved to read. Over the next few years, he would discover new authors and books, and he would be enriched by them. By 1927, he had already discovered the Puritan writings which would come to mean so much to him in future years. For example, he had received, as wedding presents, second-hand sets of books by Richard Baxter (1615–1691) and John Owen (1616–1683). Baxter was a pastor, evangelist and a theologian famous for his powerful ministry in Kidderminster, while Owen was possibly the greatest theologian among the English Puritans. These books were read avidly by the Sandfields pastor. He also relished reading about the early Calvinistic Methodist leaders in Wales and periods of revival.

Preaching

It was the Doctor's conviction that he should preach one evangelistic message each Sunday, which he did in the evening service, while the morning message was intended to instruct and encourage believers.

On 6 February 1927, his first Sunday as pastor in Sandfields, one of his sermons was on 2 Timothy 1:7: 'For God has not given us a spirit of fear, but of power and of love and of a sound mind.' The message conveyed his own burden for church members and young people who regularly attended church meetings but who were not yet converted. He appealed for honesty on their part yet recognized the difficulty of being honest with family and friends regarding one's true spiritual condition. The preacher pressed home the point. Did they question themselves as to whether or not they were real Christians? He then proceeded to provide from the text a biblical description of what constitutes a real Christian. Clearly the spiritual condition of the church itself concerned the new pastor and this needed to be dealt with before there could be an impact on the community outside.

The emptiness of nominal religion together with the dynamic intimacy and transforming character of the Christian life were emphases made regularly during those early weeks and months. In preaching evangelistically, he was at pains to demonstrate that decent morality, social and humanitarian activities, political programmes for change and reform, as well as movements advocating temperance, were not to be identified with Christianity. A miracle of regeneration must be performed inwardly in an individual by a supernatural inward work of the Holy Spirit which leads to personal trust in Christ for salvation and a transformed life.

Towards the end of February 1927, we find Lloyd-Jones preaching evangelistically from Romans 6:23: 'For the wages of sin is death, but the gift of God is eternal life in Christ Jesus our Lord.' Emphasizing the grace of God, he reassured the congregation that respectable sinners as well as the wickedest people were welcome to receive forgiveness and salvation from God in Christ. No one would be turned away and there is hope for all if they only trust in the Lord Jesus Christ.

A related emphasis in his evangelistic preaching was the brevity and uncertainty of life then the foolishness of not preparing to meet God at death. This theme was brought home powerfully in early March as he preached on the parable of the ten virgins (Matthew 25:1–3) with an emphasis on the foolish virgins. An explosion a few days previously in a South Wales coalmine in which some miners were killed reinforced his message. 'Are you ready?' was the piercing question he brought home to the congregation. Later in March, he preached on a similar theme from Hebrews 13:14: 'For here we have no continuing city, but we seek the one to come.' Exposing the church's foolishness in appealing to the world by using sport, drama and concerts to attract people to church services, Lloyd-Jones emphasized that life is a pilgrimage, and a brief one at that, so we are merely travelling through this transient world into eternity.

On Sunday 3 July 1927, a newspaper reporter, Sam Jones, attended both morning and evening services in Sandfields and wrote about his impressions. He had been attracted to the church that Sunday to hear the former Harley Street medical consultant turned preacher. He noted Lloyd-Jones' zeal and the conviction and ease with which he spoke. He found his messages 'stirring'. The morning text was from Nahum 2:1 while the evening sermon was on John 3:8: 'The wind blows where it wishes...' The preacher showed the sovereign way in which God controls all things and how humans are totally dependent on God to receive his grace and life. Sam Jones was deeply impressed by the preacher and recognized he had been genuinely called and gifted to preach.

Authority

The newspaper reporter was discerning in detecting the note of certainty in the preaching. To the preacher, this was a crucial point. He did not view his task in the pulpit as that of sharing his own ideas about religion or politics. His message would be radically different. Lloyd-Jones was aware that the critical, liberal theology and preaching which had prevailed in churches and seminaries for some years had undermined the reliability of the Bible and consequently rejected some of its traditional teachings such as the deity of Jesus Christ, his miracles and his substitutionary death on the cross for sin. Other teachings such as his physical resurrection, ascension to heaven, and future personal return in glory were generally denied. Preaching endeavoured to become more popular with an emphasis on reason, oratory and sentiment rather than proclaiming the foundational teachings of Christianity.

To Lloyd-Jones, this critical, 'modern' approach was abhorrent. The big and central question for him was that of authority. On what basis do we believe and teach anything? Is it on the authority of reason and science? Or is it based on what the church says? Or is the authority our experiences or the statements of important people or even alleged 'prophecies'? He had only one answer. The Bible is God's inspired, therefore, reliable book in which he has revealed himself and his purpose in deeds and words which are recorded accurately in Scripture by the Holy Spirit. The Bible is therefore without error. What the Bible says, God says. And that is why the newspaper reporter detected the note of authority and certainty in the preaching of Lloyd-Jones. He had a divine authority in proclaiming God's Word.

Such an approach to the Bible in his preaching was not popular with some church ministers or denominational leaders. And as the young preacher was increasingly invited to preach mid-week in other churches, he was often aware of antagonism from some ministers who were present and sitting near to the pulpit. He received a mixed reception from them, although the ordinary people in the congregations gave him a good hearing.

Preparation

However, preparing for preaching in his own church was extremely demanding, even for Lloyd-Jones. As we have already noted, reading the Bible, prayer and preparing himself, as well as two sermons, filled most of the week in his study. Prayer was central in his life, as he endeavoured to know the Lord better and to seek his power and help for preaching. He also believed in what he referred to as the 'givenness' of a text or a Bible book for preaching. Choosing a text or passage for preaching was not a random or casual exercise for him but one in which he expected the Lord to direct and provide. This again was an urgent matter for prayer that such texts and messages would be given to him.

What was the impact of this preaching on the church? Were prayers answered? These questions will be addressed in the next chapter.

6

POWERFUL PREACHING

For the first six months of his ministry in Sandfields, there appeared to be no conversions. In July 1927, one person wanted to join the church on professing conversion yet this was an isolated case. The numbers on Sundays were increasing slowly and attendance at weeknight meetings began to improve, but there was no need to use the gallery seating for about eighteen months.

Then in October 1927, the church secretary, E. T. Rees, was saved under the Doctor's preaching. A close bond had developed between Rees and the new pastor since his first visit to preach in the church the previous November. He had stayed in the Rees' home on that occasion and had thoroughly enjoyed the conversation and friendly banter they had had. A strong friendship developed in which Lloyd-Jones greatly valued the support and encouragement the church secretary gave him, referring to him as a 'practical visionary'.

E. T. Rees was a schoolteacher but actively involved in politics as a strong supporter of the Labour Party. He regarded political involvement as essential if the hundreds of miners' children in the area in urgent need of clothes and food were to be helped. Despite Rees' close relationship with his new pastor, he had not understood the gospel which was being preached. Later, he likened himself to Nicodemus in John 3 who had been ignorant of the Holy Spirit's work in regenerating sinners.

God's dealings with Rees reached a climax, however, when Lloyd-Jones was preaching on the words of John the Baptist: 'Are You the Coming One, or do we look for another?' (Matthew 11:2–5). The preacher showed how John the Baptist had misunderstood what Christ's mission was and imagined it was geared to an earthly, political programme of deliverance. That Sunday evening, 2 October, Rees was converted and went immediately to Lloyd-Jones to describe what had happened. His conversion was the beginning of more church members and adherents coming to trust the Lord Jesus Christ over the following months, as well as those without any church links.

Bethan Lloyd-Jones

Among those converted from within the church membership over the first two years was the preacher's own wife, Bethan Lloyd-Jones. Bethan had become a church member in London at the age of twelve but was confused about the gospel. The thought of God frightened her, and she was afraid to die. While she believed the Bible, attended church regularly and now supported her husband in his ministry, she did not know the grace and power of God in her life. Bethan had accompanied Martyn on his second visit to preach in the Sandfields church in December 1926. On that occasion, Martyn preached on the conversion of Zacchaeus from Luke 19. The message was uncompromising as the preacher insisted that all people were sinners and in urgent need of salvation. She felt uncomfortable and even frightened by the message. Gradually over the months she felt the guilt and burden of her own sin and was deeply unhappy. One day, Martyn gave her John Angell James' *The Anxious Enquirer Directed* to read. This was an immense help, showing her clearly that Christ's death was sufficient to cover all her sin.

As more people from different backgrounds were converted, Bethan was excited but also envied these people. Her own testimony was that in the first two years in the Sandfields church, 'God graciously used Martyn's morning sermons to open my eyes and to show me myself and my needs. I came to know my sins forgiven and the peace of God in my heart.'

Between 1927 and 1930 a considerable number of other church members were converted. Peggy Robson, a member who had previously attended a Candidates Class, came through in 1930 to a personal and saving faith in Christ. But as the months went by, there was remarkable power in the preaching with many local people being converted, including some of the town's more notorious characters.

Church growth

Church membership figures for 1928 stood at 196 which included seventy-four new members 'from the world', that is, those who had no church affiliation or involvement of any kind. This showed a net increase of fifty-one over the previous year. The 1927 membership had also shown a significant increase.

The procedure for accepting people into membership of the church was a simple one. Immediately after the end of the evening gospel service, it was the church's tradition to have a brief 'after-meeting'. Here, the pastor gave an opportunity for anyone who wished to become a church member to indicate this by raising their hand. He made no appeal and there was no pressure at all for people to respond, neither was there singing nor music in this meeting. Those indicating they wanted church membership would be interviewed privately by their pastor who then enquired concerning their spiritual experience. Lloyd-Jones had discontinued the practice of a class for prospective church members as he felt it was unhelpful and often those attending felt no spiritual concern and lacked an experience of forgiveness and new life.

Throughout his ministry there as pastor, he was available to speak to individuals not only after Sunday evening services but also following the weeknight meetings. For that reason, too, he would often be late arriving home in the evenings. Then there were a number of pastoral visits he made to needy members which he would make, often accompanied by one of the male members or officers.

By late December 1929, allowing for deaths, transfers and those leaving (seven) or expelled (eighteen), the total membership was 247. The number of church members increased significantly each year. As pastor he reported to the Annual Church Meeting in early 1931 that '84 new members had been received during 1930, 17 had been expelled (having proved themselves unworthy of membership) and membership at the beginning of 1931 was 311.'

A year later, the pastor reported to the church that during 1931, '135 men and women had been received into membership — including 128 from the world...' with eleven expelled. This meant a total membership of 424 in early

1932. The numbers of people converted 'from the world' peaked in 1931. On the opening Sunday evening of March 1931, Lloyd-Jones preached an unforgettable message from Isaiah 55:8–9: "'For My thoughts are not your thoughts, nor are your ways My ways," says the LORD. "For as the heavens are higher than the earth, so are My ways higher than your ways, and My thoughts than your thoughts."' At the after-meeting that evening, as many as fifteen people requested church membership on confession of faith.

In 1933, as many as sixty-seven were saved 'from the world', making a membership of 520. A decline in the number of those admitted into membership 'from the world' is shown for the following years with thirty-eight in 1934 (bringing the membership to its highest total of 526), thirty-two in 1935, twenty-six in 1936, and only fourteen brought into the church 'from the world' in 1937.

An analysis of all the membership figures for the period of Lloyd-Jones' ministry in Sandfields reveal that 1931 and 1932 were exceptional years in his ministry there. Some have used the word 'revival' to describe what happened locally within those few months of extraordinary blessing.

Local conversions

Amongst the many converts admitted into church membership were some interesting and notorious characters, some of whom are described by Bethan Lloyd-Jones in her *Memories of Sandfields.*

In one Fellowship Meeting, William Nobes related how he had become a Christian. In his middle age, he had a dream in which he was hanging over the raging fires of hell. He felt helpless as well as desperate; each attempt to escape failed, and he fell further and further towards the inferno. Eventually, when all hope seemed to have gone, he saw a light and a face which looked on him with amazing pity and love. Then a hand held him tightly and rescued him from the horrors below and placed him on firm ground. His consequent love for the Lord was deep, and he shared his faith most naturally with everyone.

Another trophy of grace was Mark McCann, a proud man who drank a lot and enjoyed a fight with almost anyone. He was quick-tempered and violent. One Sunday, on returning home from drinking, he cut his dog's head off because it had started eating his dinner! Remarkably he started attending the Sunday evening service and after the second visit, he remained behind for the after-meeting to indicate that God was dealing with him. He was saved that evening and his life radically changed.

Staffordshire Bill, or his real name William Thomas, which he used after his conversion, was a short, fat pensioner who often got himself drunk. One Sunday afternoon as he was drinking in a club with friends, he overheard someone talking about 'The Forward' and the preacher there. One of the men reported that he had attended the previous Sunday evening and heard the preacher say that there was hope for all, no matter how bad people were. He reflected on those words and on the third attempt was able to enter the church one Sunday evening. God dealt with him during the preaching of the gospel and, in the after-meeting, he indicated that he wanted to enter the church. The pastor, aware that God was at work in his life, said to him, 'Stand up, Mr Thomas, and let them see the latest monument to the grace of God.' Despite trials and doubts in his life, he sought to be faithful to the Lord until his death.

Testimonies

As a general norm, Lloyd-Jones did not like Christians giving their testimony as to how they were saved. However, he made an exception for Peggy Robson in 1930 when, as a church member, she was converted and was asked by the pastor to testify in the after-meeting. Nevertheless, for Lloyd-Jones, testimonies generally suggested a similar pattern, whereas there is a variety and unexpectedness in the ways in which people come to Christ. There is no stereotypical pattern. Another factor which troubled him with testimonies is that they tend to emphasize the dramatic and more carnal aspects, even misrepresenting the ways in which God had sovereignly worked. Just as serious for him was the fact that testimonies frequently draw more attention to people rather than to the grace and power of God in their lives. And if any convert referred to 'giving up' things in order to become a Christian, then Lloyd-Jones felt it was a denial of the gospel. In becoming a Christian, we receive everything and do so freely by the amazing grace of God. Conscious, too, of the way some Christians emphasized the experiences of joy, peace and satisfaction they had in believing, he warned that converts to cults also used similar language but for radically different reasons. What was important, however, was the changed lives and personal testimony of Christians in their families, employment and neighbourhood.

There is no doubt that during 1930 and 1931 there was a remarkable degree of power and freedom in the pastor's preaching. No gimmicks had been introduced, but a greater emphasis on prayer had been made and growing numbers were attending the church prayer-meeting. One remarkable prayer-meeting was held early in 1931. Lloyd-Jones had

asked an older convert, Harry Woods, to read Scripture
and to pray. He read from John 17 and then prayed with
such passion and power that it seemed as if the man was
already in heaven. Within seconds of sitting down after
praying, Harry Woods collapsed and fell to the floor, dead.
This incident had a huge impact on the congregation and
marked the beginning of an unusual spiritual quickening
of believers. Lloyd-Jones, too, was aware of this quickening
and of a greater spiritual reality in his own life.

It was in such a context that the church became even
more conscious of God's presence in their midst, so their
pastor continued his evangelistic preaching. His messages
were based on individual Bible texts taken from the Old and
New Testaments. Whatever the text, however, the gospel
was preached in a relevant, urgent and powerful manner.

In the next chapter, we will describe briefly the church
life in Sandfields and how Lloyd-Jones was led to another
sphere of ministry.

7

IN DEMAND

As increasing numbers of people came to the Sunday services, it became necessary for people to arrive as early as an hour before the commencement of a service in order to guarantee having a seat. Similarly the prayer and fellowship meetings were moved to the church building in order to cope with the numbers attending. After a couple of years, Bethan Lloyd-Jones reported that between 200 to 300 people were present in the church prayer meeting. The pastor himself kept a low profile in the meeting apart from announcing a hymn and inviting someone to read Scripture and pray. Between thirty and forty people would take part in prayer during the meeting. Other prayer meetings were arranged for Christmas morning, Good Friday, and even on a Harvest Thanksgiving day.

Death of Christ

In 1929, after preaching in Bridgend, a small town situated halfway between Cardiff and Swansea, the Calvinistic

Methodist church minister there approached Lloyd-Jones immediately. The minister was troubled because in the sermon Lloyd-Jones had emphasized divine sovereignty and the necessity of new birth, but the death of Christ had had little mention. Acknowledging the criticism, he began to rectify this serious weakness in his preaching. He read James Denney's *The Death of Christ* (1903) and other books which enabled him to see even more clearly the centrality of the cross in the gospel.

In a Cardiff bookshop during 1929, he discovered a second-hand copy of Jonathan Edwards' *Works* which were a delight, and he remarked, 'They helped me more than anything else'. He read many other theological and historical books during his period in Sandfields.

Medical referrals

However, life was full and demanding for the Sandfields pastor. In addition to his preparation for preaching, his pastoral work and itinerant preaching usually two evenings per week, with frequent afternoon services, there was a demand for his medical expertise.

At first the medical fraternity in the area was suspicious and avoided him. However, when he was eventually consulted regarding a case which puzzled local medics, then successfully diagnosed the condition accurately, it caused a stir among the local medical doctors. News of this spread, and more referrals were made to him both formally and informally. When his own church people needed medical advice, he provided this free of charge; but when people from outside were referred to him by their doctors he often charged a fee. This money, however, was usually given to the church to pay off its debt on the building and so became a significant source of income for the church.

Money

Channelling medical fees to the church is only one illustration of his refusal to allow money to become important in his life. He was firmly persuaded that as a pastor he should identify himself with the local people and depend only on his church salary to support himself and his family. To enable him to do this, before leaving London to start his ministry in Sandfields, he gave all his savings to his mother!

The attitude he adopted towards his church salary was therefore predictable. The Church Committee — there were no deacons or elders for several years — decided to increase their pastor's salary to £300 in the summer of 1928. However, in the committee meeting ten days later on 17 July, the Minutes read that the 'Pastor declined with thanks the offer of an increase in his salary, requesting the committee instead to make every effort to reduce the overdraft and also to increase the remuneration to visiting ministers and students'. His wish was granted.

In the Church Committee Minutes for 6 January 1933, again we read that 'An increase of salary was offered to the Pastor who graciously declined it; he stated, however, that he considered a salary of £350 per annum should be paid the pastor of a church like ours. It was unanimously agreed.'

Two years later, the Committee met on 4 October 1935 and 'Unanimously resolved that the salary of the pastor be immediately raised to £350 per annum'. However, at the next Committee meeting in December 1935, it was stated that 'At the expressed wish of the Pastor his salary was reduced to £300 per annum from 1 October 1935 and the proposed presentation to him was graciously declined by him.' Not only was he unselfish in this respect, but he recognized the poverty of many in his congregation and the struggle that the church had to pay off the long-standing debt on the building which stood at £3,000 when he started and which was cleared during his ministry. He was also concerned that visiting preachers, including candidates for the ministry, should benefit from the generosity of the church.

For many years he and his wife had little to spare from their income, yet they were both extremely generous in helping others who were in greater need, not only in Sandfields.

North America

On 16 March 1932, the Church Committee Minutes record that 'Leave of absence for one month was granted to the Pastor in order that he might visit Toronto.' This month's leave of absence, added to his month's holiday allowance, meant he would be away for a two-month period. Adequate and appropriate pastoral cover had been arranged by the pastor during his absence over the summer.

The purpose of the Toronto visit was to preach for nine Sundays at the United Presbyterian Church at the invitation of its Welsh minister, Dr Richard Roberts. This experience was a valuable one for Lloyd-Jones. His ministry was appreciated and congregations increased remarkably over the period that he was there. But there was time also for relaxation, and trips to Niagara Falls and to the countryside for fishing. The visit also involved a five-day conference in the United States at Chautauqua. No one seemed to know of this preacher from Wales, and there were as many as twenty main speakers. But the few meetings he was responsible for again impacted the conference. From a small group of a hundred people who chose to attend his first meeting, numbers increased so much that his final meeting was moved to a large concert auditorium seating six thousand, and it was full! This was the first of a number of visits he paid to this conference. It was a most enjoyable and beneficial trip to North America for him as well as for his wife and daughter.

Surprisingly, news of his Canadian visit was shared in England with readers of *The British Weekly* which exposed him to a wider Christian public, but he himself was delighted to be back in his own pulpit on Sunday 11 September, where he preached in the evening on Acts 20:21.

B. B. Warfield's writings

While in Canada, Lloyd-Jones had discovered the ten volumes of B. B. Warfield's writings, and he read them avidly when in Toronto. He was impressed by his high view of Scripture, the care taken in exegesis of the biblical text, his grasp of foundational doctrines such as the person of Christ, as well as his scholarship married to a deep spirituality and reliance upon the Holy Spirit. One of his priorities on his return to Wales was the purchase of those volumes and then an even more careful reading of them.

One cannot overemphasize the significance of Warfield's writings for Lloyd-Jones. Hitherto his strengths had lain more in evangelistic preaching as he was essentially an evangelist. Now, however, he began to see a great need for doctrinal teaching. He had been familiar for some time with Calvinism as a systematization of biblical truth and his own denomination's *Confession of Faith* (1823) had been a considerable help in this respect. It was not a systematization of Calvinism that Warfield gave to Lloyd-Jones but rather a greater appreciation of major, foundational doctrines, their inter-relationship, and the need to teach and uphold them biblically, thoroughly and vigorously in the prevailing climate of unbelief and scepticism. Another positive influence of Warfield on Lloyd-Jones was the exposure to the writings of the apostle Paul and especially the stimulation to grapple with Pauline theology in understanding key doctrines and then relating them to historical and systematic theology. The Sandfields pastor was impressed also by the way in which Warfield challenged the critical views of his day while at the same time presenting in various ways an impressive apologetic for Reformed Christianity.

Students

This development in his theology was timely in that he was being called increasingly to address ministers' conferences and Christian Union meetings for university students. Initially, though, when one of his members, Peggy Robson, was accepted for missionary work with the China Inland Mission (CIM), Lloyd-Jones was invited to speak at the CIM annual meeting in London in May of 1934. Attending this meeting were some of the leaders of the Inter-Varsity Fellowship (IVF, now called the UCCF), which coordinated and encouraged the work of Christian Unions in the university colleges in the United Kingdom. They were so impressed by his ministry on that occasion that they felt he should be approached to speak at their annual IVF conference. A young medical doctor, Douglas Johnson, eventually was assigned the task of visiting Lloyd-Jones while he was holidaying near

Aberystwyth in mid-Wales to persuade him to accept their invitation. After much discussion and also prayer, he agreed to speak in their April 1935 annual conference. While his ministry was appreciated, he himself was not impressed by what he saw of English evangelicalism, which he regarded as being superficial, lacking in seriousness as well as in theological and historical awareness. He noticed too the preoccupation of English evangelicals with evangelism whereas he himself was even more persuaded that only an outpouring of the Holy Spirit in revival would change the situation both in the churches and in the country. He felt the burden to urge believers to pray even more for revival.

Llangeitho again

While several meetings and factors impressed upon him the need for revival, possibly it was his preaching in Llangeitho in mid-August 1935 which also contributed. He had been invited by the South Wales Association of the Calvinistic Methodists, or its newer and more formal name of the Presbyterian Church of Wales, to preach in order to remember the bicentenary of the conversion of Daniel Rowland.

There was considerable excitement and anticipation on the part of the people who wanted to hear Lloyd-Jones preach. Unusually larger numbers arrived so that the service was moved from the church building to a marquee able to seat six thousand people. Even then hundreds of people were unable to obtain a seat and stood outside, so an estimated seven thousand people heard the Sandfields pastor preach from Acts 2:38: 'Then Peter said to them, "Repent, and let every one of you be baptized in the name of Jesus Christ for the remission of sins; and you shall receive the gift of the Holy Spirit."' The sermon emphasized the major doctrines of the gospel such as the sinfulness, guilt and condemnation of all people before a holy God, the brevity of life and the certainty of death but also of eternity; the death of Christ for sinners as the only basis for salvation and the necessity of repenting faith in the Lord Jesus were also highlighted. It was uncompromising, direct and, for many, uncomfortable. Warning his hearers to flee from the approaching wrath, he encouraged them to come to the Lord Jesus for forgiveness and to be clothed with the righteousness of Christ and then to be filled with the Holy Spirit.

There was a solemnity marking the response of the congregation after the service. For the *Western Mail,* it was 'one of the most remarkable services in west Wales since the revival of 1904'. Only eternity will reveal the full impact of that sermon.

Wider ministry

More and more invitations came for Lloyd-Jones to preach in England and in other parts of the United Kingdom, including a Sunday preaching engagement in Westminster Chapel, London, in April 1936. In May 1937, he made his second visit to North America to speak in various churches and at a conference on evangelism. It was during this trip that Dr Campbell Morgan, the minister at Westminster Chapel, London, heard him preach again and this led, in June 1937, to another preaching engagement in London, at the chapel.

Unsettled

It was a few months later that he began to feel unsettled in his Sandfields pastorate. Outwardly, there was no reason for this because his ministry continued to be effective and the church greatly valued his preaching and pastoral care. It was as if a curtain was coming down on his Sandfields ministry and this became a more settled conviction on his part. He was upset at the thought of having to leave his congregation whom he had come to love deeply; but there were also several objective factors which may have influenced him at this time. He was exhausted in the work of preaching and pastoring the church. Then there was the extensive itinerant preaching he did mid-week in various parts of Wales which added to his fatigue. He was also having trouble with his voice. Finally, there were regular calls for his medical advice that added to his workload. For these reasons, he accepted an invitation to preach on the opening Sunday of 1938 in Marylebone Presbyterian Church, London. This church was looking for a new minister and within a short time issued a unanimous call to Lloyd-Jones to become their new minister.

Lloyd-Jones himself was attracted to the church, and he thought that it may be God's guidance for him to accept. However, leaders in his own denomination in South Wales pleaded with him to stay in Wales and within the denomination. He explained to these leaders the advantages, as he saw them, of a move to London. He explained that his ministry in Sandfields was now complete, and it would be impossible for him to accept another church in the Principality and to face all the demands again of a heavy itinerant ministry. He also felt that the London church could become a centre for evangelical preaching which could have a wide influence, but he did not want to resign from his denomination.

These leaders in South Wales then suggested a different post in the denomination as there would be a vacancy within two years in their seminary in Bala for a principal and to specialize in pastoral theology. They wanted him, therefore, to consider that option. With this in mind, he declined the call to London and waited. The church at Sandfields was delighted to hear that their pastor had declined the call, but in a church meeting held at the conclusion of a Communion service on 18 May, 'To the profound regret and sorrow of the church, the pastor announced his resignation on the grounds of ill-health.'

Leaving

Unexpectedly, Lloyd-Jones received an invitation to serve in a temporary capacity as an assistant to Dr Campbell Morgan in Westminster Chapel, initially for a period of six months. He accepted the invitation with a start date for early September 1938.

'Leaving Sandfields in 1938 was not easy,' wrote Bethan Lloyd-Jones, but 'we sensed that we were being led step by step. We did not see everything clearly, but we were walking by faith.' God would be faithful in directing them into an even more fruitful and exciting sphere of ministry.

8

THE WAR YEARS

At the end of July 1938, with all the packing completed in the Sandfields home, the Lloyd-Jones family left for a much needed holiday near Aberystwyth. From their Welsh holiday, the family travelled to London and stayed with Mrs Lloyd-Jones senior, as the Doctor only expected to be assisting in Westminster Chapel for a few months.

However, from September 1938 to 1943, Lloyd-Jones assisted initially on a part-time basis, and then, in April 1939, he became associate pastor with Dr Campbell Morgan until the latter retired in 1943. He was then unanimously appointed the sole minister of Westminster Chapel. His influential London ministry continued until March 1968 when he underwent major surgery and formally retired from the pastorate. We now need to fill in some of these details to appreciate what led to his permanent appointment at Westminster Chapel.

Challenges

The five years between the autumn of 1938 and 1943 were challenging in many ways for Lloyd-Jones. Still feeling tired and unwell, he began his part-time work assisting Campbell Morgan in September 1938. He usually preached in only one of the Sunday services. Again, this was for him a temporary arrangement, although the church itself increasingly felt that his appointment should be a permanent one.

Another challenge facing him was that of itinerant preaching. He was now well known in England and pressure for him to preach in mid-week meetings both near and far became considerable. By early summer 1939, Lloyd-Jones was feeling even more exhausted than he had done a year previously and, after addressing an International Conference of Evangelical Students in Cambridge, which was sponsored by the IVF, he left with his family for a two-month summer holiday in Wales.

Then there was the matter of his future ministry. Would it be in Wales, London, or even elsewhere? He had not been certain but when urged by a deputation from the South Wales Association of the Presbyterian Church of Wales to consider a possible appointment to the Principalship of the denomination's seminary in Bala, North Wales, he had declined the earlier invitation to pastor the church at Marylebone, London, in order to make himself available to serve his denomination. His theological stature and compelling preaching made him a likely appointee for an academic post in the denomination. He had lectured in this seminary in 1933 on preaching and pastoral work; and his own outstanding ministry in Sandfields for over eleven years was also well known.

Opposition

Nevertheless, as already noted, there was considerable op-
position to Lloyd-Jones' theology by ministers and churches, even within his own denomination. The Presbyterian
Church of Wales is comprised of three Associations of
churches — one in South Wales to which Lloyd-Jones belonged, another in North Wales which was much more liberal and unsympathetic towards Lloyd-Jones, and a third
Association of the East, the latter comprising many English-
speaking churches. It was the Association in the south
which heartily recommended his appointment to the post
of Principal at Bala. The result was controversy between the
two Associations in the north and south over the issue with
the north Association successfully blocking the appointment. The newspapers in Wales also reported the affair and
criticized the denomination for not appointing Lloyd-Jones.

By the Spring of 1939, he began to feel uncomfortable
concerning the whole affair and knew that a decision was
required from him concerning accepting a more permanent
position in Westminster Chapel which had already been
offered. In late April, Campbell Morgan was able to report
to the church that Lloyd-Jones had agreed to become an
associate pastor with him in the chapel. Bethan Lloyd-Jones
related how her husband had been at peace concerning the
developments over these months and was waiting to see
how the will of God would unfold for his ministry.

Accommodation

Now that he had a permanent position as associate pastor at
the chapel, plans were made to buy a family home in London.

However, World War II was declared on 3 September 1939, and a day later Lloyd-Jones was resuming his preaching in Westminster Chapel. He had travelled alone to London while his family stayed in Wales temporarily. As their two daughters Elizabeth and Ann were now eleven and three years old respectively, it was unwise to take them to London where there was confusion, fear, and the constant expectation of heavy aerial bombing by the Germans. Air-raid sirens and shelters, the wearing of gas masks, the evacuation of many children and even families all contributed to the tension felt by residents.

It was not until December of that year that he was able to rent a suitable semi-detached house outside London in Haslemere, Surrey, which was sufficiently close for him to travel by train to Westminster Chapel. He had missed his family deeply, although he had written to his wife almost daily while they had been apart. His itinerant preaching engagements also meant that he had not been able to visit them in Wales as often as he wished. This rented accommodation, which they used for four years, therefore met many of their needs at this time and ensured that the family could be together far more often.

His health had not improved as expected. The continued feelings of exhaustion, coupled also with voice problems, caused him and the family concern. He put himself under his former medical chief, Lord Horder, and also obtained professional help for the correct use of his voice. This medical and professional help, along with exercise and a happy family life, meant that his health and voice problems began to improve slowly. Because of the distance to Westminster Chapel, Lloyd-Jones was obliged to stay in London at least on Saturday evenings, and sometimes longer if he was preaching away early in the week. Bethan Lloyd-Jones and the girls would then worship locally in the Congregational church in Haslemere.

Wider leadership

Resisting pressures to engage in a wider leadership of churches such as the Free Church Federal Council and the Congregational Union of England and Wales, Lloyd-Jones found that his leadership gifts were being channelled more in the direction of the student world and other evangelistic and missionary agencies.

Now an honorary President of the Inter-Varsity Fellowship from 1939 to 1942 and again in 1952, he delivered memorable annual presidential addresses and spoke in the movement's Theological Students' Fellowship conferences. His contacts with the IVF General Secretary, Douglas Johnson, also developed into a close and extremely enjoyable but fruitful relationship. Over these and later years, Lloyd-Jones was able to strengthen the IVF doctrinal basis and to secure its conservative doctrine of Scripture as well as helping to revive evangelical theology and challenge the arrogant, influential liberal theology which prevailed in churches and colleges.

In July 1941, Lloyd-Jones was one of the main speakers at a private conference near Oxford which was considering the possibility of establishing a centre for biblical and theological research. Hardly any evangelical academics were teaching theology or biblical studies in university faculties in the United Kingdom at that time but present at this conference were F. F. Bruce, then teaching Classics at Leeds University, and W. J. Martin, lecturing in Semitic Languages, Liverpool University.

In his address, he highlighted the dominance of liberal theology before proceeding to expose the evangelical tendency of divorcing evangelism from biblical scholarship. He felt there was an urgent need for well-trained people to answer liberal scholars in a competent but consistently biblical manner. Lloyd-Jones observed that English evangelicals had neglected both their own church history and, more importantly, biblical theology and accurate exegesis. These had been regarded by many as being 'too heavy', while the stress on the imminent return of the Lord Jesus had also lessened the sense of need for biblical scholarship. Further meetings and discussions took place which eventually led to the formation of Tyndale House in Cambridge.

One of the burdens for Lloyd-Jones, however, was evangelism and the need for the Holy Spirit to empower the proclamation of the gospel. Not only in churches and conferences but in Oxford University in 1941 and 1943 and other student meetings he preached evangelistically and powerfully.

The extent of his involvement in this period is remarkable. He encouraged, then supported, the formation of the Evangelical Library with its 25,000 books in 1943, which formally opened in January 1945. He exercised an influential advisory role in the affairs of the library and regularly spoke at its annual meetings.

It was in this period, too, that 'The Westminster Fellowship' began in 1941, primarily for ministers and others in positions of Christian leadership. Later, it was restricted to ministers. There was an emphasis in these meetings on discussion, and subjects were often practical and experimental. But as chairman, his aim was always to stimulate the men to think biblically and to learn how to apply biblical principles to the various subjects handled. Numbers were small at first but gradually increased.

In 1942, Lloyd-Jones was invited to become the first Principal of the London Bible College which opened in 1943. Although he declined the invitation, he supported the project and became the Vice-Chairman of the College Council in 1943. He was instrumental, too, in the eventual appointment of Ernest Kevan, a Strict Baptist pastor, to the post of college principal, and there were close links between the college and Westminster Chapel for a few years in which his influence on staff and students was considerable.

Other areas of involvement included the China Inland Mission which was strengthened through his respect for and fellowship with its Home Director, Fred Mitchell. In addition to speaking at many of its meetings and addressing missionaries on furlough, he also became a member of the CIM Council from 1945 until 1959 when the pressures of his work made it impossible for him to continue.

By the mid-1940s, Lloyd-Jones was heavily involved in various important expressions of evangelicalism, and he was being regarded increasingly as an important leader, advisor and speaker.

Sole pastor

In July 1943, Dr Campbell Morgan informed the church of his retirement as pastor. He was eighty years old and preaching even one sermon on a Sunday had become extremely demanding for him. Having served the church for twenty-four years, he himself was relieved and delighted that Lloyd-Jones was continuing a biblical ministry in the church.

However, the transition from being associate pastor with limited responsibilities to that of sole pastor was far from easy for him. The ministry of the Word would now become more demanding. In addition, there were members, even deacons too, who preferred Campbell Morgan and disliked the Calvinism as well as the penetrating biblical preaching of Lloyd-Jones.

Following the long summer holiday in Wales with his family, on his first Sunday back on October 3, he preached from 1 Corinthians 2:2 in the morning and then began a series of twenty-five sermons on 1 Peter in the afternoon service. He also preached five pertinent sermons during October and November on Acts 2:42. He insisted that these words provided a pattern for church life that is both biblical and urgent. Prayer, he added, is foundational to the life and work of the church. He had started a church prayer-meeting a year earlier and arranged for it to be held before the morning service in winter and before the later service in the summer.

New home

Attendances at the services increased, partly due to the presence of more Armed Forces personnel in the locality but also the return of some Londoners who had previously taken their families to safer areas of the country to avoid the bombing. It now appeared somewhat safer and the Allied Forces were making good progress in the war.

Due to the kindness and guidance of a deacon in his church who was also a builder, Lloyd-Jones was shown a rented house in Ealing, London, which proved ideal for their needs. It was in November 1943 that the family moved into their London home which meant that there was no longer need for him to travel to and from Surrey regularly. Family life was extremely important for him and to be together in London was a further encouragement. Bethan Lloyd-Jones had proved herself a wise and much loved pastor's wife in Sandfields and in the early period in Westminster Chapel. Now she could settle with the family in the church again and support her husband. He and Bethan were married for fifty-four years. His two daughters Elizabeth and Ann brought him and his wife great joy as well as, eventually, their six grandchildren.

In their new location they were kept safe, although the bombing of London was severe in the summer of 1944 when V1 and V2 bombs inflicted considerable damage on the city, with many casualties. Westminster Chapel was also damaged in this period so that a different venue was used for services over a fourteen-week period.

Thanksgiving

News of Germany's unconditional surrender and 'Victory Day in Europe' were celebrated on 8 May 1945. The following morning a thanksgiving service was held in Westminster Chapel led by their pastor. Only a few days later, on 16 May, Campbell Morgan died, and his death represented the end of an era of a distinctive but broader type of evangelicalism.

A new chapter was now opening under Lloyd-Jones, and a more vigorously biblical and Calvinistic expression of evangelicalism would emerge, which we will trace later.

9

SETTLED AT LAST

In the early summer of 1945, Lloyd-Jones had the pressing problem of finding a new family home. The house they had rented since November 1943 in Ealing was being sold and at a price he could not afford. Once again his deacon friend and builder identified a suitable house nearby which the church would rent for their pastor. With their move completed, on 30 July, Lloyd-Jones took his family to west Wales and then on to Bath in south-west England for a most enjoyable holiday.

Returning to London, many challenges and opportunities for ministry lay ahead of him, but he still lacked certainty as to where that ministry would be exercised. One factor was that neither the wider church situation nor evangelicalism in England attracted him. The latter was characterized by levity, a suspicion of theology, and a superficial message as well as evangelistic methods which he found inconsistent with Scripture. He observed that the miracle of regeneration and the need for spiritual power for gospel preaching were not generally appreciated by evangelicals. Nor was Lloyd-Jones convinced at this stage that he should continue

indefinitely in his London pastorate. He was open to the
will of God but also longed for his homeland and wondered
whether he would be led back to work in Wales.

Re-establishing the chapel

Initially, he needed to devote attention to encouraging
and re-establishing Westminster Chapel after the difficult
experience of the war years. Most of the military personnel
who had worshipped there had left military service, while a
number of the original members had decreased significantly
through death and other reasons. Those pre-war members
who remained tended to be elderly; however, there was
an increasing number of new people attending who were
attracted by the pastor's preaching. In 1945, there was a
congregation of only 500, and as a result there was need
to re-establish the church and to bring the people together
more in fellowship and unity.

His approach was clear. The preaching of the Word
would continue to be central in the church's life. In this way
believers would be established through the Word and unbelievers saved. He continued his practice of preaching one
evangelistic message per Sunday which would be on Sunday
evenings. But Lloyd-Jones was convinced from Scripture
that preaching without the power of the Holy Spirit would
achieve little. The God-ordained way of obtaining success
in such preaching was prayer arising from a deep sense of
dependence on the Lord for him to work through the Word.

He prepared well for his preaching and began to introduce
more series of expository sermons yet making each sermon
complete in itself. For example, between October 1946 and
March 1947, he expounded 2 Peter in the morning services

while in October 1946, he undertook a series of evangelistic messages from John 3 followed by messages from Isaiah 35:1–8.

The Word was beginning to have an impact on the congregations so that towards the end of 1946 there was considerable encouragement with the 'steady increase in the size of the congregations' but, more importantly, 'the conversion of many souls'. He could report to his daughter Elizabeth later in this period that the Sunday evening service 'was a night of much conviction'. On another occasion he wrote to his daughter: 'Several came to see me at the end. It was certainly a night of much convicting power and I felt I was being used...' But he made no appeals for people to come forward, and there was no emotional pressure placed on the congregation. He believed it was the work of the Holy Spirit to give new life and to bring sinners to faith in Christ.

The integration of members and adherents into church life was further encouraged by an 'At Home' meeting each autumn where folk could mix more freely with their pastor and his wife. He also encouraged more frequent church-member meetings and, after concluding the business of the church, he requested that a missionary should address the members.

Fellowship and discussion

Lloyd-Jones then introduced a Friday evening 'Fellowship and Discussion'. He attached considerable importance to this meeting, which was an opportunity not only for anyone to ask a question concerning the Christian life, but also to ask questions of a practical and spiritual nature. Usually the questions emerged from the circumstances and experiences of the believers themselves, and afterwards maximum discussion was encouraged by those present. His aim was for the people to identify and apply biblical principles to their situations and problems.

Once the questions were agreed upon, there was lively discussion and helpful leadership followed by excellent summaries from Lloyd-Jones with as many as 200 attending in the beginning. An extensive and helpful range of subjects was covered in these discussions. A sample of the questions includes: How can God's will be recognized? What is saving faith and how does it differ from a more theoretical acceptance of gospel doctrines? Are our lives planned by God? Can tiredness and illness legitimately be regarded as factors which make sin less significant in our lives? What is the minimum amount of Bible knowledge a person needs to become a Christian? Why are some Christians less successful in personal evangelism? Can a person be both carnal and a Christian? These Friday evening meetings facilitated closer fellowship within the chapel and by the autumn of 1948, the Institute Hall where it was held was overcrowded.

IFES

Alongside his Westminster Chapel ministry and his regular itinerant preaching throughout Britain, Lloyd-Jones gave an increasing amount of time to ministry amongst international students. One of his first visits was to Norway in September 1946 and then to Boston a year later in order to address a conference at which the International Fellowship of Evangelical Students (IFES) would be formed. After 1947 when he spoke for IFES at Lausanne, there followed several years of active support and travel for the movement where his contribution was enormous. He was the chairman of IFES from 1947 to 1957, then president until 1967. He provided IFES with a strong, theological base and encouraged national leadership in the various countries where it operated.

Settled

A letter to church members in January 1949 in which Lloyd-Jones reflects on the work during 1948 provides some helpful insight into his own feelings and thoughts. There are five details here which are important. First, he confirmed that 'many have been brought to a saving knowledge of the Lord Jesus Christ'. He thanked God for this, recognizing it as a divine work. Second, he emphasized that 'We do not press for decisions as we know that the Holy Spirit alone can do the work'. That was consistent with what he had taught and practised over the years. Third, he allowed a more personal reference to the effect that 'I am increasingly conscious of being surrounded and supported by a truly spiritual fellowship'. He felt encouraged and strengthened in his work by their prayers and work. This suggests that measures taken earlier to strengthen the bonds between members, and to foster closer ties between pastor and people were bearing fruit. Fourth, the chapel was no longer a mere preaching station. And fifth, Lloyd-Jones was now beginning to feel more settled in the work. 'As to the future,' he wrote, 'I feel more and more that we have been called and set by God to witness together here in the heart of London.' Gone now was the feeling of being unsettled or wondering where he might serve in the future.

One factor in giving him a more settled conviction was that the door to a post in Wales had closed by 1947. There had

been a possibility of him being appointed as Superintendent
of the Forward Movement of the Presbyterian Church of
Wales. And Lloyd-Jones had been open to the possibility with
its emphasis on evangelism and church planting. However,
as in the case of Bala, he was not appointed but instead they
appointed his brother-in-law, Ieuan Phillips! Whether Lloyd-
Jones would have accepted the post if offered, or fitted into
the work of the Forward Movement are now only hypotheti-
cal questions. He was sure that God guides often through
closing as well as opening doors for service.

Other factors contributing to his assurance of being in
the right place must have been the extensive blessing on
his preaching ministry and the way in which Westminster
Chapel was being moulded into a more prayerful and closer
fellowship. Unlike the earlier years, he felt that he was now
embraced and supported by the whole church. Under God,
the blessing would continue and his influence would expand.

Widening ministry

Ministry outside the chapel for Lloyd-Jones became even
more demanding. In addition to his mid-week preaching
in churches in various parts of the country, he was also
being used more locally by various evangelical agencies.
The London Inter-Faculty Christian Unions used him for
an evangelistic mission in 1947. Later that year he was
speaking in the Great Hall of King's College, London, for
the Christian Union. At this later meeting, the chairman
was R. V. G. Tasker, Professor of New Testament Exegesis
at the University of London. In the Professor's introductory
remarks, he referred to an occasion three years previously
when Lloyd-Jones had spoken in that same hall and 'when

his own life was revolutionized by that address'. Staff as well as students were converted through his preaching.

The Graduates Fellowship of the IVF also called upon him to speak, as did the Christian Medical Fellowship formed in 1949. From 1953–1968, he chaired a monthly Medical Study Group which produced some helpful publications.

In 1948, the Scripture Union (formerly the Children's Special Service Mission) republished his *Presentation of the Gospel*. This had originally been published in 1942 by the Crusaders' Union, which also specialized in evangelism amongst children and youth. This published address had considerable influence amongst those engaged in evangelism. For Lloyd-Jones the subject was important because the churches were failing to preach the gospel and as a result there was godlessness and materialism in the nation. He urged those involved in evangelism to regard the glorifying of God as their supreme motive coupled with a reliance on the Holy Spirit who works through the Word of God alone. There were many dangers for them to avoid, too, such as the exalting of the 'decision'.

Calvinism

Back in 1944, he had delivered a radio address for BBC Wales on John Calvin in which he noted that a 'great change' had occurred in theology over the previous twenty years in terms of the greater attention being paid to Calvin. He attributed this largely to the influence of Karl Barth, even though he disagreed with Barth on some doctrines like that of Scripture.

What attracted Lloyd-Jones to Calvin was that 'he bases everything on the Bible', not reason, and affirmed that 'the great central and all-important truth was the sovereignty of God and God's glory'. In creation, providence and salvation God is sovereign, so all humans are sinful and guilty before God, unable to save themselves. In his grace, God planned, accomplished and applies salvation by his Spirit to the elect whom he keeps and sustains until they enter glory. All these truths were regarded by Lloyd-Jones as being thoroughly biblical. Having recommended to the publishers of James Clarke and Co. that they should publish Calvin's *Institutes of the Christian Religion,* he was delighted when they appeared in 1949, and he commended them heartily to the Christian public.

The emphasis by Lloyd-Jones on divine sovereignty, however, isolated him from some evangelicals in England; but that was not by his choice. While holding tenaciously onto Calvinistic teaching, he rarely used the term himself and did not believe that Christians should argue or separate over it.

But there were many, nevertheless, who desired to be taught in the Word and who came to rejoice in the sovereignty of their triune God through his ministry. An example of this will be provided in the next chapter with regard to students in Wales.

10

A BETTER BALANCE

There was concern once again over Lloyd-Jones' health in the early summer of 1949. He felt exhausted and suffered from catarrh as well as other ailments such as depression due to overwork. Wisely, he decided to seek the medical advice of his former hospital boss, Lord Horder. The latter had no doubt that Lloyd-Jones needed a prolonged period of rest. Lloyd-Jones had a trip planned for July and August in the United States with a punishing speaking schedule in churches and conferences. Lord Horder directed that the trip should be cancelled in order to secure the necessary rest. His advice was accepted so at the end of June Lloyd-Jones took his wife to west Wales. The following weeks were significant for many reasons.

Joy and light

Part of the summer break included several days residence during July at a clinic near Bristol where he had treatment for catarrh. He spent much of the fortnight on his own in a private room while his wife and family returned to London for a few days. Not only was he unwell but, in addition, he had been struggling for some time with a temptation to question, against his will, the support of an important friend whom he valued. He had no evidence for doubting this friend yet these powerful, negative thoughts contributed to his darkness of soul and depression.

Early one morning he sensed evil in his room and experienced 'complete agony of soul'. He knew the devil was near, but as he dressed, the situation changed dramatically. One of Arthur W. Pink's sermons lay open alongside his bed and his eye suddenly fastened on the word 'glory' on one of the pages. Suddenly, he felt surrounded by God's presence and the love of God was poured into him, giving him amazing assurance and degrees of joy and light he had never known before in his Christian experience. For a number of days this overwhelming joy stayed with him.

It was an experience he did not write about and rarely referred to. He never gave a label to it. However, he regarded it as a genuine experience of the Holy Spirit in which he was given a deep certainty concerning his own personal salvation and an intense, intimate enjoyment of the Lord.

In late July, the whole family went to stay on a farmhouse near Bala. Still tired and listless, it took several days for Lloyd-Jones to regain any vigour. But on a Saturday evening in the farmhouse, he was alone reading the hymns of a famous Welsh hymn-writer, William Williams (1717–1791), when he knew God's felt presence and the reality of his love. This experience seemed greater than even on the first occasion in the Bristol clinic. The realities of the gospel and of heaven became gloriously real to him once again.

New emphasis

In his biography of Lloyd-Jones, Iain Murray suggests that these two experiences represented a new phase and emphasis in his ministry. He is correct. Reflecting much later on these events, Lloyd-Jones acknowledged that they were 'a real turning point' in which he found a better balance between the doctrinal and experiential aspects in his preaching.

The following days and months confirm this fact. For example, with little warning some Christian students sought his help while he was holidaying at this time in North Wales. He had met the students earlier in the year when he had preached evangelistically for them in Bangor University. Now these same students were providing an evangelical witness for the first time in Wales's National Eisteddfod, an annual Welsh language cultural festival which attracts thousands of people. The festival rotates between North and South Wales, and on this occasion it was held in Dolgellau, near to where Lloyd-Jones and his wife were on holiday.

He agreed to help by speaking informally to the students before a meal then preaching powerfully late that evening on Philippians 4:4 to a large congregation. His meeting was reported the following day on BBC Wales and Mrs Lloyd-Jones senior was surprised to hear her son had been preaching when he was supposed to be resting! The remaining holiday included a refreshing couple of weeks in Ireland.

He and Bethan were back in London in good time for him to preach in Westminster Chapel on Sunday 11 September. There was a problem, however. All his attempts to prepare a message for the Sunday morning service had failed, and it was only as he was in prayer on the Saturday afternoon that the words from Titus 1:2 came to his mind most powerfully: 'God, who cannot lie.' It was an unforgettable moment, and he was overwhelmed as the sermon was given him in outline. He was given exceptional power and freedom in preaching the following morning and the congregation were made aware of the glory and presence of God.

Wales IVF

A few days later he returned to Wales to address the first Welsh IVF Conference which was held near Aberystwyth. About sixty students attended and Lloyd-Jones devoted three addresses to the subject of the biblical doctrine of man. For the student chairman, it was a remarkable three days with many students expressing appreciation of the Word. He addressed the conference again in the 1950 Easter vacation, this time on the doctrine of the Holy Spirit. Many students discovered for the first time that, prior to any decision and repentance on our part, the beginnings of grace must be traced to the Holy Spirit's miraculous work in regenerating the sinner.

The third Welsh IVF conference was in July 1951 when Lloyd-Jones responded to a request to speak on divine sovereignty. He delivered three powerful addresses on the subject, warning students that the subject should be approached from the Bible rather than from a prejudiced 'Calvinist' or 'non-Calvinist' position. The effect of these talks on the students was extensive and permanent. Some were converted, others struggled before submitting to a more God-centred theology, while others came to a deep assurance and joy in the Lord. Because he did not want the students to depend on him, this was the last Welsh IVF conference that he would speak at.

There were other developments taking place in Wales, especially the emergence of the Evangelical Movement of Wales, largely through these students and conferences for Welsh language believers. Lloyd-Jones also spoke at their pioneering conferences in 1953 and 1955.

Ministers' conference

Then in 1955, evangelical ministers within the Presbyterian Church of Wales established a ministers' conference for their members at which Lloyd-Jones was invited to speak. He accepted the invitation but only on condition that evangelical ministers from other denominations were invited to attend. This was agreed upon and for the first time evangelical ministers from different denominations conferred together; it was a milestone in expressing evangelical unity. His ministry on the Holy Spirit in this conference had a major influence on ministers. Between 1955 and 1978, Lloyd-Jones attended the majority of these conferences in order to lead the discussions and give the closing message. His influence again was considerable as he instructed, encouraged, challenged and also pastored these ministers over the years.

Expository preaching

It was during the 1950s and 1960s that Lloyd-Jones preached some of his most outstanding expository series of sermons

on Sundays in Westminster Chapel and on Friday evenings.
Amongst the better-known series are the six sermons in 1950
on Habakkuk *(From Fear to Faith)* and sixty sermons on *The
Sermon on the Mount* from 1950–1952. Just as influential
was the long series on John 17 (*The Basis of Christian Unity*)
in 1952–1953, Psalm 73 (*Faith on Trial*) in 1953–1954, and
twenty-one sermons on *Spiritual Depression: its causes and
cure* which were preached from January–July 1954. October
1954 saw the commencement of his Sunday morning
exposition of *Ephesians* which consisted of two hundred
and sixty sermons spanning a period of eight years, ending
in July 1962. His memorable Bible studies on *Romans* on
Friday evenings started in October 1955 and ended only
when he retired due to illness in March 1968.

He described all these sermons and studies as 'expository',
which he believed all preaching should be. By this he meant
that the preacher needed to indicate initially the relevance of
the verses and then explain what they mean in their context.
However, expository preaching demands even more than
this, for the preacher should then open up and apply the
doctrine. That was what he himself endeavoured to do in
expository preaching.

Experimental

Lloyd-Jones wrote a brief article for the Evangelical
Movement of Wales' Welsh language magazine (*Cylchgrawn
Efengylaidd*, January–April 1950) expressing his desires
for the year 1950. It was a moving article that revealed the
longings of his heart for even greater spiritual reality than
he had hitherto known. 'Before everything else', he affirmed,

'my chief desire is "to know Him".' He knew how easy it was to be satisfied and content with teaching or defending the faith or enjoying peace and joy in the Christian life. These things are the privileges of believers. However, to know the Lord more intimately was his great longing and also for the church to experience a great revival that year.

Bethan Lloyd-Jones referred to the fact that her husband was first of all a man of prayer and an evangelist. He spent much time seeking and enjoying the Lord in private prayer. There were many times in London in the fifties and sixties when the Lord drew so near to him that he needed to leave the study and talk to his wife in the kitchen about very mundane matters like the lunch menu. He did this, he explained, in order to reassure himself that he was still on earth and not in heaven! No wonder that as he prayed and preached in the Sunday services, people were often made conscious of God's glory and presence as well as the power and authority in his preaching.

Throughout this period, this note of knowing God was emphasized more and more both in his preaching at the chapel and in churches and conferences outside. For example, he told the evangelical ministers in Bala, Wales, in 1964, 'My greatest problem is not to prepare my sermons but myself. And the only way is by a personal intimate knowledge of Him. Our supreme desire must be to have communion with Him.'

Evangelism

In the late 1940s and throughout the 1950s there was considerable blessing on evangelism both in churches and in the universities in various parts of the United Kingdom. Lloyd-Jones himself was preaching evangelistically on Sunday evenings and also in churches and universities throughout the country on a weekly basis. People were being converted through his ministry near and far, including many who would be called to preach themselves or to serve as missionaries.

One unusual occasion which he seized was when he was invited to address the Christian Medical Fellowship over a meal during the British Medical Association's annual meetings in Cardiff in 1953. All the doctors in the BMA meetings were invited to hear Lloyd-Jones speak on 'The Doctor himself'. He had prepared an address relevant for the occasion, but he felt troubled about what he had prepared and instead preached from Luke 12:13–21 on the parable of the 'rich' or 'successful' fool. Preaching the gospel faithfully and powerfully but with deep compassion, he showed how foolish doctors are if they make no preparation for their own death.

Harringay 1954

There was considerable excitement in London and the provinces when Billy Graham, the world-renowned evangelist, and his team came to London for an eleven-week evangelistic mission in 1954. While disagreeing with their approach to evangelism and its emphasis on public 'appeals', the number of 'converts', the prominence of testimonies and its weaker theology, Lloyd-Jones still prayed for the meetings and was open to see what the Lord would do. He also refrained from public criticism and personally helped some members of the Harringay team. But the Christian press and public seemed excited by the Harringay meetings, the 37,600 people who attended, and also the significant numbers 'going forward' in response to the 'appeal'.

There were three main reasons why he refused to cooperate in the mission. One important reason was that non-evangelical church leaders were invited onto the public platform at these Harringay meetings. Those leaders invited were among the many church leaders who denied many foundational gospel truths. He felt that it was wrong as well as misleading to use them in this way and to suggest that they were on the side of the gospel.

Another reason was the use of 'appeals' after the message. He believed that this interfered with what the Holy Spirit was doing in the lives of people. To use a choir while the preacher pleaded with the congregation to respond to Christ by 'coming to the front' and making a 'decision' was wrong. This was for Lloyd-Jones a man-centred emphasis which deceived people into thinking a physical action like going forward made them a Christian. Thirdly, and related to this, it assumed a weak understanding of the work of the Holy Spirit who alone regenerates a sinner. In this action, the Holy Spirit gives new spiritual life in what is an inward and radical work which cannot be accomplished by physical means or by 'pressure' from an evangelist or a choir.

Amongst the clergy and pastors in south-east England, Lloyd-Jones was in a minority and was frequently misunderstood over the issue. But there were other pressures and changes taking place as well, which were to challenge him and his leadership amongst evangelicals in England.

In the next chapter, we will use the lens of Lloyd-Jones to see how he understood the situation and identified the religious changes taking place at that time.

11

A CHANGING SITUATION

For some years, Lloyd-Jones had been troubled concerning the shallowness of English evangelicalism and its aversion to doctrine. This was a longstanding problem, dating back to the nineteenth century and the formation of the Evangelical Alliance (EA). The result was that a broad expression of evangelicalism had developed in the twentieth century which tended to minimize doctrine. Now, the major changes afoot in Christendom with the neutral response of the EA raised major issues like, 'What is a Christian?'; 'What is a church?'; and 'What does the Bible teach about Christian unity?' These questions raised basic questions concerning the fundamental truths of Christianity. And Lloyd-Jones showed that churches which had imbibed liberal theology and sacramentalism would get the answers to all these questions wrong.

In order to sketch the main issues and developments during the 1950s and 1960s, we need to recognize some important dates.

1948

After several years of preparation, the World Council of Churches (WCC) was formed in Amsterdam in August 1948. Many Protestant church denominations, and later Orthodox churches, joined on the basis of a brief but vague statement of membership. Theologically, the WCC had mixed views concerning the gospel. The purpose of WCC was to pursue a wide, visible expression of unity and cooperation. Divisions and disunity were regarded as the major reason for the ineffectiveness of churches, at least in the West.

This 'new' situation was serious because nearly all the church groupings in the United Kingdom were prepared to accommodate one another in order to achieve mergers and cooperation in various ways.

For Lloyd-Jones, this major move for unity was not based on the Bible and did not safeguard the biblical gospel. To the crucial question, 'What is a Christian?' these churches would have given radically different answers. They had, therefore, a wrong view as to what Christian unity was.

1956–1961

In October 1954, Lloyd-Jones, along with a few other evangelicals such as Leith Samuel, was invited by the British Council of Churches to join a consultation for those with differing views of the Bible. The purpose? To explore whether cooperation in evangelism was possible, irrespective of their doctrinal differences. Lloyd-Jones accepted the invitation and attended all twenty-one consultations.

The first one was delayed until November 1956 when sixteen members were present. It was assumed by some present that the only difference between them was the doctrine of the Bible. However, Lloyd-Jones queried this and recommended that in their next meeting they should discuss first the doctrine of Christ's death. This was agreed upon, and he himself provided an opening statement on the subject for the next meeting in February 1957. Emphasizing that Christ was a substitute for sinners when he was 'made a curse for us', he highlighted as a matter of necessity the character of God and God's holy wrath against sin. No forgiveness is possible, he insisted, unless the divine wrath is satisfied. 'Propitiation', therefore, was necessary before God could pardon sin. Most of those present opposed his position. Other subjects in the following meetings included 'New Life in Christ', 'The Church', 'Justification by Faith' and 'Man in Sin'. Fundamental differences of opinion emerged each time within the group concerning foundational biblical doctrines, centring on the character of God. Numbers attending had declined so the BCC decided to end the consultation.

What is remarkable is the considerable amount of time and effort Lloyd-Jones had devoted to attending and pre-paring for these meetings. What had they achieved? They had shown conclusively that it was impossible to cooperate in evangelism with those who deny basic gospel doctrines. They were not differences which could be ignored or dealt with lightly.

1962–1965

All the Roman Catholic bishops were called to Rome for the Vatican II Council and discussions were arranged in blocks of several weeks over the period of 1962 to 1965. The council had been called by Pope John XXIII who had become pope in 1958. No one expected him to be anything but a caretaker leader, but within five years he had changed the Roman Church in various ways. His aim for the council was pastoral because he wanted his people to adapt to the new world situation and the challenges facing the church.

Some of the decisions that he made there were radical. For example, Protestants were now regarded as 'separated brethren' rather than as heretics, and they would encourage their people to read the Bible in the vernacular. They acknowledged that people outside their church, even in Islam, could be saved, and an inclusivist theology was endorsed. The Bible, too, was now regarded as part of the evolving church tradition. Altogether, this council moved Roman Catholicism further away from biblical teaching, and it still denied the doctrine of justification by faith alone.

What Lloyd-Jones observed correctly was the changing attitude also of Protestants, including an increasing number of evangelicals, towards the Roman Catholic Church in which there was sympathy and active cooperation in various ventures. Gospel distinctives were now blurred in what was becoming a broad coalition. Some evangelicals were prepared to ignore the Protestant Reformation and the cardinal doctrines it rediscovered.

1966

Lloyd-Jones was invited by EA leaders to repeat in public what he had shared with its commission concerning unity. He did so at the National Assembly of Evangelicals meeting in the autumn of 1966 in London. His address has been debated, analysed and interpreted endlessly by Christians and theologians; and different positions have been taken concerning it. In order to clarify what he said, the following question and answer approach may make it easier for readers to grasp the main principles and issues.

Q: What was the title of his address?

A: The title was 'Evangelical Unity: An Appeal'. Notice that it was preoccupied with unity, not secession. His emphasis was on evangelicals *associating* or *uniting* but on the basis of the gospel as taught in the Bible.

Q: Why choose this title?

A: Because Christians were in a 'new situation' due to the formation of the WCC, and unity was the 'major fact confronting us'. Church denominations were consequently prepared to reconsider their positions. Evangelicals therefore had a unique opportunity, one they had not had before, to express gospel unity.

Q: What were the main issues raised by Lloyd-Jones?

A. What is a Christian? That was the first issue. Among those pressing for church unity, there was no biblical agreement on the answer to this foundational question. Only those who believe personally in the Lord Jesus Christ alone for salvation belong to the true church, Lloyd-Jones rightly insisted.

Q: What was the second issue?

A: This second issue concerned the nature of the church. What is the church? Arguing from Acts 2:42 ('And they continued steadfastly in the apostles' doctrine and fellowship, in the breaking of bread, and in prayers'), the Westminster Chapel pastor argued that those pushing the church's agenda for unity put fellowship and cooperation before doctrine, whereas evangelicals must, like the early church, place doctrine first. So before there can be genuine spiritual unity, there must be agreement on doctrines such as the Bible, the person of Christ, his virgin birth, sinless life, miracles and his final, penal, substitutionary death for sinners, his physical resurrection, his personal return in glory as well as the person and work of the Holy Spirit. These doctrines are essential for salvation.

Q: Finally, what did Lloyd-Jones want to achieve?

A: He certainly did not want one united evangelical church. Nor did he want to be its leader either. He did want an 'evangelical ecumenicity'. For evangelicals to remain separate from one another in different denominations where false teaching was prominent and tolerated, made them guilty of 'schism'. But, he probed, 'Do we not feel the call to come together, not occasionally, but always?'

For Lloyd-Jones, we are guardians and custodians of biblical truth and modern successors to those principled men who fought for this same gospel in earlier centuries. Was the Protestant Reformation under Luther and Calvin a mistake? If not, why do we not stand for the gospel today?

The chairman of the meeting, Rev. John Stott, immediately disagreed with Lloyd-Jones and urged ministers to stay in their denominations. *The Christian* (21 October 1966), a weekly newspaper, claimed that many people present in the meeting agreed with Lloyd-Jones but that no action would be taken until leaders like John Stott gave a lead. That was not an option now and a deep cleavage opened up between evangelicals in the Anglican and Free churches.

To what extent, if at all, was Lloyd-Jones responsible for this division? Opinion on this question is still divided. Some claim that he was unwise and hard in his attitude. Remember, however, that he was asked to repeat this address to the public. It was neither his plan, nor his wish to do so at this time. Nor did he publish his address so misconceptions as to what he actually said became common.

More seriously, Lloyd-Jones had no definite plan as to how this wider, permanent expression of gospel unity was to take shape. That was possibly his weakness. His preference had been for a large umbrella type of association of gospel churches where there could be differences on secondary issues. This would provide togetherness in the gospel which would be permanent and visible to the world. Having dealt with the major biblical principles, Lloyd-Jones expected others to assume the initiative and to offer a detailed way forward. No one did so. Another vital fact, too, is that he definitely did not want the role of leader in a new association of churches.

Keele 1967

Only six months later, in April 1967, the first National Evangelical Anglican Congress was held in Keele under the chairmanship of John Stott. The Archbishop of Canterbury, Dr Michael Ramsey, preached in the opening meeting, even though he was no evangelical, and had a liberal attitude to the Bible. In the 1950s he had criticized English evangelicalism for being 'heretical'. Ramsey was also sympathetic to the prospect of a reunion with the Roman Catholic Church.

Together with the pope, Archbishop Ramsey issued a *Common Declaration* aimed at 'a restoration of complete communion of faith and sacramental life' between their two churches. The first step was the establishment of the Anglican-Roman Catholic Joint Preparatory Council (1967–1968), out of which came the Anglican-Roman Catholic International Commission (ARCIC) from 1971 onwards. Consequently, the Keele Congress confirmed and popularized the new broader approach of Anglican evangelicals towards ecumenism. As a result, instead of expressing gospel unity as Lloyd-Jones had wanted, evangelicals in England became even more divided, a fact which deeply saddened him.

The British Evangelical Council (BEC) was established in 1952 in order to provide a more biblical expression of gospel unity for churches, in contrast to the theologically broad and mixed World Council of Churches. Following the negative response to his 1966 address, Lloyd-Jones turned to the BEC as the best option available for expressing gospel unity. When the BEC, therefore, held its first real public conference in 1967, Lloyd-Jones was the obvious choice to deliver the closing address. And he did so at eight of the BEC conferences between 1967 and 1979. It was only his ill-health which prevented him from contributing more to these conferences.

More than 2,500 people crowded into Westminster Chapel on 1 November 1967 to hear Lloyd-Jones deliver the closing address at the BEC Conference. Commemorating the 450th anniversary of Luther's writing and nailing of his *Ninety-Five Theses* to the castle doors at Wittenburg, his message was 'Luther and his message for today'. He acknowledged he was 'immensely encouraged' by the numbers present who wanted to identify themelves with

Reformation gospel doctrines. For his remaining years he encouraged and supported the BEC as it sought a wider expression of gospel unity.

Surgery and retirement

Despite the controversy he had been involved in following the 1966 address, Lloyd-Jones remained encouraged in his own church ministry and in other aspects of the work. For example, in December 1966 he informed the Evangelical Library annual meeting of his encouragement that more Christians were reading good quality Christian literature. He felt this was due to the work of the Library, the IVF and the Banner of Truth Trust.

His itinerant ministry continued to be appreciated by congregations. One special occasion for him was preaching in Aberfan, South Wales, in November 1967 to commemorate the first anniversary of the major disaster in the village when a junior school was unexpectedly engulfed by a moving mountain of coal slurry, killing 116 children and twenty-eight adults. He preached from Romans 8:18–23 and many people found great comfort and were challenged by his message.

His 1967 summer vacation was spent in North America and included a period of relaxation as well as ministry. Back at Westminster Chapel, in the autumn, he was preaching with considerable freedom and power through Acts evangelistically on Sunday evenings while in the mornings he had been preaching through John's Gospel since 1962.

His encouragement was expressed in an annual letter to church members in January 1968 as he reflected on the previous church year. There was 'a sense of expectancy' felt by many in the church services while he himself was also hearing of people regularly coming to faith in Christ. 'Thus', he reported, 'I find myself greatly encouraged.' By contrast, he referred in the same letter to the confusion and divided opinions which existed in the wider situation.

After feeling unwell for a few days, Lloyd-Jones was taken ill and was admitted to a London hospital for major cancer surgery on 7 March. He shared with his wife that he was quietly confident in the Lord that the surgery would be successful and that he would be able to resume his itinerant ministry and other interests. However, he felt that his period as pastor of Westminster Chapel had come to an end.

During his convalescence, he called a deacons' meeting on 29 May 1968, to announce his resignation as pastor. They, and later the entire congregation, were disappointed as were many others who had benefited from his preaching in the chapel.

12

A NEW MINISTRY

In retiring from his ministry in Westminster Chapel, Lloyd-Jones was certain this was God's will for him. He had no doubts about it. He and his wife Bethan continued their membership in the chapel, but they would only join the Sunday service during the first hymn and leave during the final hymn. He took no active part in the life or administration of the church.

There was another matter he felt certain about, namely, that he was beginning a new ministry. From now on he would concentrate on itinerant preaching, the preparing of his sermons for publication, and encouraging younger pastors. The latter he would achieve partly by preaching in their churches mid-week or at weekends. These, together with continued support for a few evangelical agencies, would be his priorities over the thirteen years which were ahead of him.

Many of the members and deacons at Westminster Chapel rejoiced at these new priorities, especially because many more people would now be able to enjoy the messages they themselves had heard.

Westminster Fraternal

There was considerable joy and excitement felt by the ministers belonging to the monthly Westminster Fraternal when Lloyd-Jones joined them in their meeting on 9 October 1968, for the first time since he became ill. On this occasion, he shared in a personal way his experiences during his illness and convalescence over several months.

Lloyd-Jones considered it appropriate and divinely planned that he had finished his Friday evening studies in Romans 14:17, prior to having surgery. This was important to him and also a considerable challenge. The verse reads: 'for the kingdom of God is not eating and drinking, but righteousness and peace and joy in the Holy Spirit.' His last study had been on peace but then, he claimed, 'God intervened.' While he knew much about the peace of God, he felt God wanted him to experience more about 'joy in the Holy Spirit' before speaking on it.

He explained that for four months during convalescence he had listened to preaching, but that he had found the services 'terribly depressing.' And there was little 'joy in the Holy Spirit' in the services. Identifying himself with others, he stressed that people in the congregation were often desperately in need of help, encouragement and grace. He felt that preachers were too professional and intellectual, with 'no life, no power.'

A further observation he made on the preaching he heard was that too many men gave a 'running commentary' on a Bible verse or passage, which he insisted was not preaching. There must be a message arising from the principles of the verse which are to be proclaimed with authority, relevance and power. There was for him a 'lack of power' in preaching.

Extensive ministry

In addition to his itinerant ministry in churches, in November 1968, he addressed the annual meeting of the Evangelical Library and then, a few days later, the annual BEC Conference in Liverpool where his subject was, 'What is the Church?' At the Puritan Conference (later renamed the Westminster Conference), during the following month, he spoke on 'William Williams and Welsh Calvinistic Methodism'. During March 1969 he spoke at two important medical meetings as well as the annual IVF Conference. It was a heavy schedule.

USA trip

Lloyd-Jones and his wife, Bethan, then went on their final visit to the United States and enjoyed a period of five-months' ministry there. This allowed time for relaxation and sightseeing as well as renewing friendships. There were many preaching engagements in churches and conferences waiting for him and his ministry was greatly appreciated. One of the main reasons for the trip, however, was to give sixteen lectures on 'Preaching and Preachers' in Westminster Seminary, Philadelphia. These lectures were delivered over a period of six weeks. In 1971, the lectures were published under the same title, *Preaching and Preachers*. This is one of his most important and influential books, and it is valuable too for the way in which Lloyd-Jones draws extensively on his own experience. They returned to England in early September feeling refreshed and stimulated.

Books

He honoured his commitment to prepare his sermons for wider circulation in book form, and spent a great deal of time editing the manuscripts of his Westminster sermons. Others were involved with him in this arduous task, but he himself made the important editorial decisions.

Between 1970 to 1975, he prepared several volumes of Romans for publication, with a new volume being published each year. The first one to appear was *Atonement and Justification* (Romans 3:20–4:25) in 1970. But why start the series with this section of Romans? He explains the reason in his Preface: 'The answer is that I am anxious to proceed at once to what may be called the "heart" of the epistle.' Lloyd-Jones enlarged on this and gave three further reasons. First, the vital theme of justification by faith is worked out in detail in these two chapters. Second, the verses show that there is only one way of salvation. Third, it emphasizes that the gospel is entirely God's for he plans, he initiates, he sends, he accomplishes, and he applies salvation. He also describes Romans 4:4–5 as 'one of the most important verses in the whole of the Bible ... from the stand-point of evangelism ... and of becoming a Christian.'

The Ephesians series first appeared in 1972 with *God's Way of Reconciliation* (Ephesians 2:1–22).While there was some apprehension whether the Christian public would buy such relatively substantial and expository books, sales were mostly encouraging. For example, in the first ten years of the appearance of these volumes, more than one million copies were sold.

Growing into union

Division and confusion are words which continue to describe
English evangelicalism during the 1970s. Lloyd-Jones had
been troubled for some years by the way in which many
English evangelicals who claimed to embrace foundational
doctrines like the supreme authority of the Bible were
prepared to tolerate and cooperate in denominations with
those who interpreted these doctrines very differently.
Keele 1967 was one glaring example for Lloyd-Jones when
Archbishop Ramsey was invited to address Anglican
evangelicals. He observed with sadness his Anglican
brethren being drawn into an ecumenism where gospel
distinctives were being compromised.

Another painful example of this compromise for him was
a publication in 1970 entitled *Growing into Union: Proposals
for Forming a United Church in England*. This was written by
four Anglicans, two of whom were Anglo-Catholics and two
were Evangelicals, one of whom was James Packer. What
was disturbing was the insistence by all these authors that
both the Evangelical and Anglo-Catholic views must coexist
together in the proposed united church. And there was a
firm commitment by the authors that they would continue
together in this conviction, despite what their close friends
and supporters said.

The implications of this approach were far-reaching
and Lloyd-Jones saw this. For example, the tradition of the
church was being given equal status to that of Scripture.
The Bible was no longer supremely authoritative. Just as
disturbing were claims that regeneration by the Holy Spirit
occurred in baptism, making the child a saved person. The
place of bishops was also emphasized as being essential.

Criticism of the book from Anglican evangelicals was muted, but for Lloyd-Jones such radically divergent views meant that his previously close working relationship with Packer ended. The Puritan Conference of which Packer had been a strong supporter for years was closed down.

Other books were published by Anglican evangelicals supporting the rather new involvement in a broad ecumenism more tolerant of heresy. In 1973, a second book by Anglican evangelicals, *Evangelicals Today*, was strongly critical of the evangelicalism of the past, particularly in the way it had answered the question, 'What is a Christian?', and the way it encouraged attendance only at evangelical churches.

But in the 1966 address and his response to *Growing into Union*, he had refused to compromise the gospel. That was why he had appealed to evangelicals to express their gospel unity rather than remain in mixed denominations with those who denied the gospel.

Charismatic movement

The undermining, and even the disparaging, of key Bible doctrines was also illustrated for Lloyd-Jones in the emergence and growth of the Charismatic movement from the early 1960s. Some people had been genuinely helped within the movement in terms of believing in Christ and enjoying a more intimate relationship with the Lord. A number of emphases they made were helpful in drawing attention to the gifting and involvement of all believers within the church, an emphasis on prayer and warm, loving relationships amongst believers with a concern for the needy and disadvantaged.

In the early 1960s, the Charismatic movement taught, like classic Pentecostalism, post-conversion Spirit baptism, speaking in tongues alongside revelatory and miraculous gifts. By the late 1960s, however, the movement had become more theologically diverse. What further differentiated the Charismatic movement from Pentecostalism was the deliberate policy of working within the various denominations, even if liberal and sacramentalist. Gradually, Spirit baptism was perceived by many as being more important than justification by faith alone, and a theological vagueness developed with regard to the gospel itself. Consequently, the movement began increasingly to converge with ecumenism and was adapted by Roman Catholics.

In his studies in Romans early in 1966, Lloyd-Jones had warned his people of these trends and dangers. He continued to sound out such warnings as in, for example, the IFES conference in 1971. 'Nothing matters', he told the students, 'not even important gospel doctrines "but the baptism of the Spirit". The great thing is that you have this experience … doctrine does not matter at all.' He condemned that teaching. Addressing the BEC Conference in 1977, Lloyd-Jones acknowledged:

Until about ten years ago we were engaged in this fight alongside other evangelicals in the mixed denominations. But now the situation has taken a very sad and a very tragic turn... When I spoke in 1966 I was aware of certain trends and of certain tendencies, but in my wildest moments I never imagined that things would take place which have actually come to pass during these past ten years — almost incredible.

While addressed primarily to the Anglican evangelical leadership, his remarks applied generally to those trends which undermined the gospel and weakened the resolve of those evangelicals who wanted to safeguard that gospel.

For Lloyd-Jones, the gospel and its proclamation was the most important thing. And preachers ought to prepare well for this demanding task and to pray often for God's help and blessing. That is what he taught pastors and that is what he did by example, even during these years of controversy and disappointment.

The gospel was everything to him. We will not, therefore, understand his 1966 address or subsequent responses to ecumenism, liberal theology, or the Charismatic movement unless this fact is understood.

13

GLORY ANTICIPATED

The editing of his preaching material for publication continued unabated during the 1970s but so did his itinerant preaching ministry. One must not underestimate the extent of his regular preaching throughout the United Kingdom in 1970 and onwards. He was in considerable demand as a preacher and was prepared to travel great distances, usually by train, to fulfil his engagements. A significant number of engagements were in Wales, but he was also a frequent visitor to Scotland for preaching and holidays. He preached in large city meetings, but he was also happy to preach in small and more discouraged churches in order to help pastor and people. This was an invaluable ministry.

Despite the snow and the national coal-miners' strike which was in progress, Lloyd-Jones preached in February 1973 in the mining valley of Maesteg in South Wales. Church membership was under one hundred, but the local town hall mid-week was crowded both afternoon and evening for the two preaching services. It was a huge encouragement for the local pastor and his people. The gospel was powerfully preached and a sense of God's presence and glory was felt even by unbelievers.

Lloyd-Jones was accustomed to encourage a pastor in his home as he enjoyed hospitality. He would be relaxed as he reminisced concerning his own ministry and sought to understand what the Lord was doing in that local situation. There was always the promise that he would pray for the pastor and his family. Occasionally a phone call would reassure the pastor of prayer support and Lloyd-Jones would be overjoyed to hear of conversions. This was an aspect of his ministry to which he attached a great deal of importance.

Again when that same pastor moved to a different pastorate two years later, Lloyd-Jones was eager to travel a considerable distance to preach twice in his induction services over the weekend. He was a pastor of pastors and, despite his stern appearance, he was a kind, generous and approachable man who was deeply concerned for younger pastors.

Pastors would renew fellowship with him in conferences such as the BEC or the Evangelical Movement of Wales Ministers' Conference in Bala each year, or in the monthly Westminster Fraternal. He was available to listen to the problems men would share with him and to give his advice. That advice at times could be unpredictable and even surprising, though it was not always heeded. But he shared his deep concern that gospel work should continue and that a new generation of pastors should be supported. It was in that context, and recognizing the need for the biblical and practical training of such men, that Lloyd-Jones eventually agreed that a new independent seminary — called the London Theological Seminary — be established in England's capital city. This was opened on 6 October 1977, and he delivered the inaugural address.

Restrictions

After preaching in early February 1979, it was necessary for him to cancel his engagements until September that year. He had succumbed to a viral infection in his lungs and later required minor surgery. Back in 1976, he had undergone surgery a second time for cancer, but in 1979 there were symptoms which suggested that it had returned.

However, he resumed his preaching in September 1979, and in November he preached the closing address for the BEC Conference in London. This was the last time he would speak for the BEC and also the last occasion in which he was to preach in his old pulpit at Westminster Chapel. But he preached powerfully from Matthew 22:21: 'Render therefore to Caesar the things that are Caesar's, and to God the things that are God's.' His emphasis was clear. As the Pharisees were preoccupied with lesser things, in the same way churches face the same danger. Taxes, money and all its benefits are all passing and uncertain, he insisted. They cannot help people to die and to face God. He then went on to emphasize that the benefits which God freely gives are incomparable and eternal. 'He gave His only Son. Nothing I know is more glorious than the death of Christ for sinners.'

Death

Lloyd-Jones expressed to Iain Murray in early March 1980 his conviction that during the months of weakness and sickness he was being given time to prepare for death. He regarded it as very important. This was to be one of his main tasks over the next months. 'We are too busy', he observed. 'The world is too much with us. We hold on to life so tenaciously — that is so wrong, so different from the New Testament!'

Not having preached since December, he was well enough, though extremely weak, to preach to a congregation of 700 in Carlisle in north-west England on Sunday 4 May, and then on the following Friday in Glasgow to mark the Jubilee of the Scottish Evangelistic Council. The occasion gave him considerable joy as he had first preached for the Council in 1942.

His health was deteriorating slowly, but he preached occasionally over the following few weeks. In June, it became necessary for him to go into hospital for a few days every three weeks for treatment, but he was at peace and also content, knowing he was in the Lord's hands. His time was short but he read books and hymns, prayed and meditated on the Word, and longed for more of the reality of the Lord's presence.

During these final months, his family continued to be a great support and comfort to him. Bethan and his two daughters, Elizabeth and Ann, were at hand. During late February 1981, he became even weaker and was unable to speak. Refusing antibiotics to ease his condition, he scribbled on a piece of paper for the family: 'Do not pray for healing. Do not hold me back from the glory.' His wish was granted, and he died on 1 March 1981.

Five days later he was buried in west Wales, outside of Newcastle Emlyn where a large number of ministers and believers were in attendance. There was a deep sense of loss felt by all present.

On Monday 6 April, Westminster Chapel was overflowing with 2,500 people for a thanksgiving service in honour of the life and work of the Doctor. Five different speakers referred to his contributions in the fields of medicine, student ministry, Christian literature, Westminster Chapel, and, finally, as a preacher. To close the service, a message from Revelation 1:17–18 reminded the congregation of the glories of Christ, the one whom Lloyd-Jones had loved, preached and served so faithfully and passionately. It was a most moving occasion and one which pointed not only to the various gifts and contributions of this remarkable man but also to God's grace which had been so evident in his life.

Worldwide influence

His ministry had touched many lives worldwide. Thirty years after the death of Dr Martyn Lloyd-Jones, it is impossible to describe adequately his extensive influence on churches, individuals and preachers outside the United Kingdom. More of his books, cassettes and DVDs have become available and are widely distributed through various publishing houses, such as the Martyn Lloyd-Jones Recording Trust.

His sermons are also broadcast with some of these programmes available on the internet at www.oneplace.com which claims to be the world's largest internet radio station. Many books authored by Lloyd-Jones have been translated into other languages, including Spanish, Portuguese and Korean. In these ways his powerful ministry continues and, possibly, even increases today.

14

LEGACY

In this closing chapter, we remind ourselves of what Lloyd-Jones believed and then we will indicate some of the challenges of his ministry and the legacy he has bequeathed to us.

His beliefs

We have seen that Lloyd-Jones believed and preached the Bible. All his printed and audio material confirm this fact. For him, the Bible is the supreme authority in all matters of faith and practice.

Following the end of the war in 1945, the Doctor held weekly discussion meetings in Westminster Chapel to discuss varied practical questions relating to the Christian life. These meetings were popular and well attended. It was during these discussions that the Doctor recognized that his people needed a firmer and more detailed grounding in the teachings of the Bible. Consequently, for three years, from 1952–1955, he gave a series of talks on major biblical doctrines. Many people found these talks extremely valuable in enabling them to understand and appreciate what was taught in the Bible.

Our interest in highlighting these doctrines is to confirm what Lloyd-Jones believed. One can turn to many of his books for this purpose, but we refer to these addresses he gave between 1952–1955. You will find the outlines of these doctrines in published form in *Dr Martyn Lloyd-Jones: Great Doctrine Series, God the Father, God the Son* (vol.1), *God the Holy Spirit* (vol.2), and *The Church and the Last Things* (vol.3) published by Hodder. They are readable and helpful books for Christians.

What then did Lloyd-Jones believe?

The Bible

He believed that the Bible is God's Word. In the Bible God has revealed himself and his purpose in the words and deeds recorded accurately there. For that reason, the Bible must be supremely authoritative for Christians and churches. Reason, philosophy, experience, the tradition and teaching of the church and its leaders as well as personal views must all be subject to the teaching of God's book.

In different ways, Lloyd-Jones challenged the arrogant expressions of reason and the secular philosophy of his day. He knew that a new critical approach to the Bible from Germany had gained ground since the mid nineteenth century and had substituted reason or philosophy for the Bible. The consequences were tragic, as major biblical doctrines had been rejected or modified in many church denominations. Here, however, was a brilliant medical scientist with a string of medical degrees who reaffirmed the authority of the Bible as God's Word, over and above reason, experience and even the church. He stood unashamedly for biblical doctrine, whatever another minister or congregation might think.

For Lloyd-Jones, the following facts were determinative in establishing the inspiration and authority of the Bible: the Bible's claims concerning itself, the superintending work of the Holy Spirit ensuring that the human authors were 'carried along' by the Holy Spirit to write only what was accurate, and then 'the most vital testimony' of the Lord Jesus who quoted, believed and taught the Old Testament Scripture. Consequently, in the Bible we have 'the record of God's greatest redemptive acts ... also God's comment upon those acts; God's exposition of them; God's explanation of the way of salvation as well as the unfolding of the way itself. And the Bible claims that it and it alone has this revelation — there is no other. If God does not reveal Himself, I cannot know Him; but He has revealed Himself, and that revelation is to be found in this book.'

Throughout his ministry Lloyd-Jones refused to compromise the Bible's central focus on Christ and redemption. For example, he preached one evening in the Rhondda Valley, South Wales, during the 1950s on the glory and uniqueness of Christ as the only one able to save sinners. It was a powerful message. Immediately after the sermon, however, the church minister stood up to announce the closing hymn, but first he announced that he disagreed with the preacher. He insisted there were several ways to be saved apart from Christ. Following the singing of the hymn, Lloyd-Jones moved forward to give the benediction but first told the congregation to sit. For several minutes he then showed the congregation from the Bible that there is only one gospel and only one Saviour, namely, Jesus Christ. Apart from Christ, he insisted, there is no salvation.

What Lloyd-Jones did was courageous, but for him it was also necessary and important; it is the Bible, not the opinions of people, which should decide what we believe.

God

Lloyd-Jones was profoundly aware of the glory of God as taught in the Bible. God is free of limitations so he is everywhere, eternal, unlimited, in power and knowledge. He is spirit, transcendent, personal, and although one, he exists in three distinguishable persons, namely, Father, Son and Holy Spirit who are coequal and coeternal. This God is unchanging, holy and righteous in all that he does and says.

Lloyd-Jones was delighted to be able to proclaim the greatness of this God, but also his goodness and love which is shown to all creatures. And yet there is a 'still more glorious' way in which this love is expressed, namely, in loving sinners who deserve only his condemnation. That love is expressed supremely at Calvary where the Lord Jesus died as the substitute bearing our guilt and punishment. As our mediator, the Lord Jesus was then raised from the dead, and ascended to heaven where he is in session at the right hand of God the Father, ruling over the church and the world.

God plans and saves

Lloyd-Jones was persuaded that the Bible teaches God's sovereignty in creation, providence and in salvation. Throughout the centuries God has worked according to his own absolute plan, which applies to all his creatures, not just to Christians or even humans, but also to animals and angels (Ephesians 1:11). This plan involves his own choice from eternity of those who will be saved (Ephesians 1:3–6), and this is because he was pleased to do so (Romans 9:15–16). God the Father also appointed his Son to become our representative and substitute to die for the elect. To do this, the eternal Son of God assumed our human nature, while remaining God: 'This one indivisible Person, who now had two natures instead of one, chose to, and actually did, live as a man, taking the form of a servant and humbling Himself, becoming obedient ... even to the death of the cross.'

Man

Created in the divine image, sustained and entirely dependent upon God, man became a sinner due to the disobedience of our first parents, Adam and Eve (Genesis 3; Romans 5:12–19). All humans consequently are under the power, pollution and guilt of sin but also subject to divine punishment.

Application of salvation

Because all people are spiritually dead and at enmity with God, only God the Holy Spirit can give spiritual life (regeneration) and bring sinners under conviction of sin to believe on Christ for salvation. Lloyd-Jones was strong on this emphasis and also insisted that the Holy Spirit indwells believers, strengthens and sanctifies them, enabling them to pray and understand the Bible. This ongoing work of the Holy Spirit in believers is essential and effective until we reach heaven. That is why Lloyd-Jones emphasized so much the necessity of the Holy Spirit's ministry to make the gospel effective both in evangelism and in church ministry.

The church and Last Things

We have seen that during the 1950s and 1960s, Lloyd-Jones emphasized the importance of two questions, namely, 'What is a Christian?' and, 'What is the church?' The church, he taught, consists of those who believe personally on Christ and have been born again. The preaching of the Bible is then necessary for the spiritual growth and holiness of believers, providing fellowship and enabling them to live worthily of Christ in the world. There are times when God 'revives' the church, too, and gives it an unusual degree of power, spiritual reality, light as well as joy concerning gospel truths.

Personally, suddenly and gloriously, the Lord Jesus will return from heaven to consummate God's purposes; all the elect will be glorified and unbelievers will be separated from the mercy and grace of God eternally in hell.

These Bible doctrines were precious to Lloyd-Jones, and he delighted in proclaiming them throughout his ministry.

His challenge

In the words of John Brencher, Lloyd-Jones was 'an outstanding figure in twentieth-century evangelicalism'. A 'genius' and a 'great man' is the way Gaius Davies has described him. However, he was neither infallible nor perfect, consequently he continues to be criticized, sometimes unfairly. For example, his lack of formal theological training has been viewed negatively by some. Again, despite his regular itinerant mid-week preaching being appreciated by many UK churches, he is criticized for not developing his Westminster church into a more local fellowship. There is then the enigma of Lloyd-Jones himself never resigning from the Presbyterian Church of Wales, even though he had encouraged evangelicals to leave mixed denominations. While the principle Lloyd-Jones identified, namely, of withdrawing from mixed denominations was a 'sound one', as Carl Trueman has noted, his reasons for not having a 'positive' plan in that situation were weak, although understandable. His exegesis and interpretation of key biblical texts regarding Spirit baptism also evoked criticism as well as his cautious rejection of the cessation of extra-ordinary gifts.

These and other criticisms of Lloyd-Jones are discussed in other literature but they must not detract from our appreciation of his outstanding gifts and the massive contribution of his ministry. His life and work challenge us today. There are three main areas of challenge that will be underlined here.

Word and Spirit

One of the greatest challenges from Lloyd-Jones for us today is that of maintaining a balance between Word and Spirit. But let me explain.

The divine Word, that is, the Bible, is primary and must be preached faithfully and clearly as well as obeyed. Lloyd-Jones warned ministers at the Bala Conference in 1957 that 'The Holy Spirit will not bless anything else' other than his Word. Whether in evangelism or church ministry the Word and the Word preached must be central and God-honouring.

However, in and of itself, the Word will not save anyone. To be effective, the Word preached and witnessed must be accompanied by the power of the Holy Spirit who alone is able to regenerate sinners and bring them to Christ. Lloyd-Jones established this biblically as in 1 Corinthians 2:3–5 and 1 Thessalonians 1:5. In other words, the Holy Spirit's ministry along with the Word is indispensable. He also amply illustrated this in the preaching of the early Calvinistic Methodists in Wales as well as many others like George Whitefield (1714–1770) and John Wesley (1703–1791).

The implications of this emphasis by Lloyd-Jones for us are many but three can be shared here. First, all Christians, especially preachers and evangelists, must be people of prayer, depending on the Lord fully. He is the living God and is able to save and bless, but prayer is the means which he has appointed for us to use to request his help. Second, we are challenged to develop an intimate fellowship with the living God. The same Holy Spirit who blesses and uses his Word also enables Christians to know and enjoy the Lord better. We need to know God for that is what Christianity is all about (John 17:3). Third, it is not enough to share testimonies or stories in evangelism or Sunday School teaching. It is God's Word which must be shared and taught with its central focus on Christ.

The glory of the gospel

Nothing mattered more to the Doctor than the gospel. His first text when he preached in Sandfields was 1 Corinthians 2:2: 'For I determined not to know anything among you except Jesus Christ and Him crucified.' Those words, also enshrined on his gravestone near Newcastle Emlyn, capture the burden and message of his preaching ministry over many years.

He would not allow the gospel to be compromised or endangered. That is why he referred to liberal, critical theology in the churches as 'poison', since it undermined and, in many places, destroyed the gospel and what had been for years gospel churches. This 'poison' of false teaching needed to be removed from the churches. And his 1966 appeal for evangelical unity was an appeal to evangelicals to stand by this biblical gospel together and to proclaim it to the world. How could they remain in denominations where leaders and ministers denied this gospel?

The impact of his message in 1966 was extensive and the ripples are still being felt in evangelical circles throughout the United Kingdom. Many Anglican evangelicals remained loyal to their denomination then, but a trickle of men left both before and after 1966. Many from other denominations in England and Wales left them either then or over the following years. The British Evangelical Council (now called Affinity) provided an essential link for many of these churches to enjoy a wider expression of evangelical unity.

It does need to be emphasized, however, that behind the unity issue is the unique and glorious gospel of Christ in which Lloyd-Jones rejoiced. He preached in the autumn of 1963 at Westminster Chapel on the words of Galatians 6:14: 'But God forbid that I should boast except in the cross of our Lord Jesus Christ.' As he explained what the Lord Jesus did on the cross, he seemed to be carried away with a deep sense of wonder and amazement:

I see one who is sinless ... who gives perfect obedience to his Father... I see the sinless one being punished... I see the face of one who from eternity had looked into the face of his Father... I see the Lord of glory... I see one who has such power that he can make all things... I see him dying in utter

helplessness... I see one who was in the form of God, dying
as a weak and helpless man... I see one whose concern for
the glory of the Father was so great that he put aside his own
eternal glory in its visible form and humbled himself ... and
was obedient even unto death ... what I see above everything
else is the love that made him do it all ... he is dying there
because of his love, his love for you, his love for me, his love
for ... sinners ... rebels ... enemies... I see the holy Son of
God bearing the punishment of my sins, the author of life
dying that I might live, that I might become a son ... and go
on to spend my eternity in the glory everlasting with him...

How could such a message be compromised or regarded as
a mere viewpoint within a denomination? That was Lloyd-
Jones' concern.

The need for revival

Was revival, as some suggest, an 'overemphasis' and an
'obsession' for Lloyd-Jones? Some think so, but we need to
assess what he says about revival before we can answer the
question responsibly.

What is revival? That is where we must begin. Lloyd-Jones
defined the term 'revival' as 'a period of unusual blessing
and activity in the life of a church'. From Isaiah 63:1–6, he
explained that over the centuries the church has often been
weak and lifeless. Unexpectedly, the Lord arises, scatters
his enemies, and the church is revived. The result is that
believers are quickened and given a new, deeper dimension
in their relationship with the Lord, while many unbelievers
are also saved within a brief period.

From Joshua 4, he taught that revival occurs when the
Holy Spirit comes down in power upon a number of people

or upon a church or churches. But Lloyd-Jones emphasized that revival is very different from an evangelistic campaign. Rather, revival is something which God does to the church; it is a 'special time' in the life of the church when God intervenes. And it is God alone who gives revival. No preacher or evangelist can produce a genuine revival. That is God's prerogative alone, and he is sovereign working when, where and how he pleases in revival.

But on this view of revival, does Lloyd-Jones disparage the ongoing permanent work of the Holy Spirit in believers? Not at all. He regarded the 'ordinary', ongoing work of the Holy Spirit in the believer as essential. No one can *become* a Christian without him, nor can anyone *remain* a Christian. His ongoing work in teaching, sanctifying the believer, illumining the mind concerning the Bible, leading in prayer, and empowering the preaching of the gospel are vital and necessary all of the time. There must be no disparaging of this continuous work of the Spirit outside periods of revival. The latter is only a difference in the degree and extent of the Holy Spirit's power working within the church.

For Lloyd-Jones both the Old and New Testaments taught and illustrated the fact of revival. From Pentecost onwards during the period of the New Testament Church, there were frequent outpourings of the Holy Spirit upon believers so that the apostles as well as others preached with remarkable power as the Holy Spirit accompanied their preaching.

The Doctor also knew his church history well and was impressed by the way, especially since the sixteenth century, men and churches had often known periods of revival. He knew, for example, there had been local, regional and national revivals in Wales between 1735 and 1904–1905 — on average, at least every seven years in Wales. But he was also familiar with the great works of God's revival in other countries.

Was the subject of revival an 'obsession' or an 'over-emphasis' then for Lloyd-Jones? He certainly emphasized it because he was convinced it was biblical and historically attested on many occasions. In addition, he was convinced that it was the supreme need of the church. Despite all the emphasis and activities by churches and various movements concerning evangelism in the twentieth century, the churches in the West remained weak and powerless.

But for Lloyd-Jones it was also part of a deeper problem. Addressing ministers in Bala, North Wales, in 1971, he declared: 'Life! There is a lack of life amongst us. What is the cause? It is due to a lack of realization that God is a living God. There is a neglect on our part of the living God ... What has kept the church alive is God acting in revival. Our supreme need is to realize God is alive...'

This strand in his teaching was neither an 'overemphasis' nor an 'obsession'. Rather it was the expression and burden of a man who was single-minded in taking Bible teaching and church history seriously with the supreme motive of seeing God glorified again in revival in his day.

At the 1959 Puritan Studies Conference in London, Lloyd-Jones offered reasons why Christians were no longer thinking seriously in terms of revival. Among those reasons there are two which we can highlight. One was the wrong emphasis on learning rather than on spirituality for ministers and those training for the ministry. Another reason was the influence of Charles G. Finney (1792–1875) in America who identified revival with an evangelistic campaign, and which they were able to make successful under certain conditions. This was entirely different from the way, for example, Asahel Nettleton (1783–1843) viewed revival, namely, as a divine, sovereign and intensely powerful work of the Holy Spirit.

Lloyd-Jones suggested there are these two positions with regard to revival. In the past, when troubled about the weak condition of the church and the lack of conversions and life, many pastors and church officers would call the church to pray specifically for God to visit them in power. They did that most earnestly and regularly. They relied on God alone, not on themselves or on an evangelist. By contrast, Lloyd-Jones remarked that the contemporary approach was to arrange an evangelistic campaign, choose an evangelist, and then ask God to bless their efforts. 'I belong to the old school,' he remarked. 'The campaign approach trusts ultimately in techniques rather than in the power of the Holy Spirit ... I am convinced that nothing can avail but churches and ministers on their knees in total dependence on God.'

In an interview in the *Evangelical Magazine of Wales* in 1975, Lloyd-Jones claimed: 'I think I know why God has kept an awakening or revival from us.' He gave three reasons. First, 'the Lord is seeking to bring us to our knees... We must see more clearly ... that we are completely dependent on God... He alone can empower the Word and change situations.'

Second, he warned we should not despise the day of small things. Referring to Wales and the period 1950–1975, he said, 'I believe there has been an awakening in the sense of the clearing of our minds and getting a grip on the big doctrines of the Faith and it is still happening. It MAY lead to revival.' His third reason is interesting. 'A new generation of Christians has sprung up in Wales and in the rest of the United Kingdom — there is blessing but no revival.' Then in his closing remark, he added: 'These years have been a great benefit to us; if revival comes, we now have gospel churches ready to receive the new people.'

CONCLUSION

His legacy to us is considerable. He provided an example of contemporary, biblical preaching which was compelling and powerful but gospel-centred. Tributes to him as a preacher abound. For the Rev. Eric Alexander in Scotland, Lloyd-Jones 'was the greatest preacher the English speaking world has seen in the twentieth century'. Dr James Packer referred to him as 'the greatest man I have ever known', while earlier the continental theologian, Emil Brunner, regarded him as 'the greatest preacher in Christendom'. We have now the enormous benefit of his printed and audio sermons and addresses being easily available to us to read and listen to.

In addition, Lloyd-Jones provided principles and advice from his own experience in his *Preaching and Preachers* to assist preachers in their own ministries. And for the pastors and churches, he left the conviction concerning the vital importance of biblical doctrines and the centrality of the glorious gospel of Christ. That is a valuable legacy and, if coupled now with earnest prayer for revival, then the legacy is rich indeed.

Further reading

D. Martyn Lloyd-Jones, *Preaching and Preachers* (London: Hodder and Stoughton, 1971).

D. Martyn Lloyd-Jones, *Sermon on the Mount* (Leicester: IVP, 1976).

Iain H. Murray, *D. Martyn Lloyd-Jones: The First Forty Years, 1899–1939* (Edinburgh: Banner of Truth, 1982).

Iain H. Murray, *D. Martyn Lloyd-Jones: The Fight of faith, 1939–1981* (Edinburgh, Banner of Truth, 1990).